EAST RIDING SECRET RESISTANCE

Alan Williamson

MP Middleton Press

Front Cover:

Left: Charlie Mason of South Cave Patrol stands near the entrance to Burton Agnes hide. (Author 1995)

Right: Group No. 7 is in training in Bluestone Quarry in Walkington. (Mrs A Taylor)

Lower: Interior of Bewholme Patrol hide. (Author)

Back Cover: Reconstruction drawing of South Dalton Control (Zero) Station inner radio chamber. (Simon Williamson. Copyright)

> ! WARNING !
>
> **All sites are on PRIVATE PROPERTY and cannot be visited**

Published March 2004

ISBN 1 904474 21 7

© Alan Williamson &
   Middleton Press, 2004

Design   David Pede

Published by
     Middleton Press
     Easebourne Lane
     Midhurst, West Sussex
     GU29 9AZ
Tel: 01730 813169
Fax: 01730 812601
Email: info@middletonpress.co.uk
www.middletonpress.co.uk

Printed & bound by MPG Books Ltd, Bodmin, Cornwall

Foreword

The setting up and operation of the Secret Army must rate as one of the best-kept secrets of the Second World War; and what is perhaps more surprising is that no formal acknowledgement was made even of its former existence until quite late in the 1960s. As a result, it features little, if at all, in most published histories of the period, and our knowledge of its organisation and activities in many parts of the country is at best sketchy, and for some areas is still non-existent. Nor is there a wealth of official documentation on which historians and archaeologists can draw, to help them fill the gaps in our records.

The appearance of this volume is particularly welcome, as it serves two purposes. The first is that it draws on a large number of interviews and discussions with original members of the various Secret Army units based in East Yorkshire. Alan Williamson has gone to great pains to track down the surviving members, and, where possible, to interview them in order to record their reminiscences; because of the length of time that has already elapsed since the War, and because many of these gentlemen are now in their 80s or older, it is indeed timely that this research was carried out now whilst so many participants are still available to shed light on the organisation of their particular units.

The second major contribution of this work is to record in detail the surviving archaeology of the Secret Army's bases and hides in this area. Prior to this ground-breaking fieldwork, not even the existence of a single site would have been found in the local Sites and Monuments Records Offices or in the records of English Heritage, and no national or regional guidance notes as to the range of structures that were built and used by these Secret Army units were available for study. Thus, the painstaking research and recording carried out by the author is an invaluable contribution to our understanding of these little-known sites - their remains, how they were built, equipped, and operated. The fruits of this labour will not only be used locally, but will help to guide others in recording similar structures elsewhere in the country. To date, not a single Secret Army site in England has been selected for protection as a Scheduled Ancient Monument; in the light of this work, English Heritage might well choose to include some of these sites within their Monuments Protection Programme. Many such sites have already been lost, whilst many more are currently at risk of destruction, either through development or accidental loss; hence, it is important to ensure that these little-known monuments are properly recorded, before they disappear altogether.

This has been a labour of love, and represents the culmination of over a decade of careful research and fieldwork, which sheds an unique light on a little-known aspect of recent history in East Yorkshire. This work grew out of the Defence of Britain Project, and has benefited greatly from the input of Charlie Mason. Firstly, as a surviving member of the Secret Army, he was able to give first-hand information and advice on the organisation and activities of the various units; but, secondly, he participated actively in much of the fieldwork with Alan, rediscovering and exploring the various hides and operational bases described and illustrated in this book.

Dave Evans
(Archaeology Manager, Humber Archaeology Partnership)   August 2003

From Lord Hotham

I cannot claim I have any contemporary memories of the Auxiliary units, though as a disgression I can remember watching the presentation of colours to General Leclerc's 2nd Armoured Division on the 3rd of July 1944 in front of our house.

I can however say how much I admired Alan's enthusiasm and quiet expertise. It had long been an ambition of mine to find the underground bunker here that complemented the above ground Nissen Hut that was occupied during the war by what my father referred to as the secret ATS. I do not know how much he knew about them, but he didn't tell me anything. Some limited pheasant shooting carried on during the war and my father did mention to me that he offered a pound to anyone who could drop a bird on the hut roof!

Alan inspired me to join him in a really determined search for "The Bunker" about which a certain amount of disinformation had been spread regarding its post-war destruction.

I very well remember the day we found that it still existed, we, Alan, Charlie Mason (Alan's invaluable ex. Aux Unit's helper) and I came back here and my wife produced lunch for two extra without batting an eyelid - we washed it down with a bottle or so of celebratory wine.

So thanks to Alan Williamson, another Zero Station was rediscovered and recorded.

Lord Hotham
South Dalton Hall
East Yorkshire

2 October 2003

Contents

		Page
1.	**Preface**	10
2.	**Operation Sealion**	11
3.	**Auxiliary Units**	13

   3.1   The Beginning
   3.2   Recruitment
   3.3   Operational Base
   3.4   Equipment
   3.5   Training

| 4. | **East Riding Auxiliary Units** | 29 |
| 5. | **East Riding Patrols** | 37 |

5.1   Northern Area

Bainton	Flixton	Norton
Bridlington North	Harpham	Scampston
Bridlington South	Kilham	Settrington
Burton Agnes	Kilnwick	Westow
Burton Flemin	Leavening	Wharram
		Wold Newton

5.2   Southern Area

Aldborough	Catwick	Skeffling
Beverley North	Cottingham North	Skirlaugh
Beveley South	Cottingham South	South Cave
Bilton	Hornsea	Sunk Island
Brough	North Cave	Walkington
		Withernsea

5.3	The Lost Patrol – Spaldington	87
5.4	The Mystery Bunker	90
6	**Special Duties Branch**	91

   6.1   Background
   6.2   East Riding
   6.3   The Intelligence Network

7	**The Stand Down**	110
8	**The Final Chapter**	116
9	**Appendices**	120
10	**References**	125
11	**Bibliography**	126

List of Maps and Drawings

	Page
Plan of Anti-invasion coastal defences (1941)	12
Drawing of standard Aux Unit Shelter (1941)	17
Drawing of Aux Unit OB (East Riding MKII)	22
German map of East Riding Coast (Military Geographical Targets 1940s)	28
Map of East Riding Aux Units	30
Survey drawing of Aux Unit HQ OB (Rise)	31
Survey drawing of Aux Unit HQ OB (Middleton)	35
Survey drawing of Bridlington North Patrol OB	38
Survey drawing of Bewholme Patrol OB	56
Construction drawing of Horsea Patrol OB	61
Sketch drawing of Skeffling Patrol OB	63
Survey drawing of Beverley South Patrol OB	69
Survey drawing of Walkington Patrol OB	71
Sketch drawing of Bilton Patrol OB	73
Survey drawing of Cottingham South Patrol OB	75
Survey drawing of North Cave Patrol OB	79
Sketch drawing of North Cave Patrol OB and OP	82
Sketch drawing of South Cave Patrol OB layout	86
Survey drawing of North Cave underground store	89
Survey drawing Goathland Out Stas	94
Survey drawing of South Dalton Control Zero Station	99
Computer generated drawing of South Dalton Surface Zero Station	102
Survey drawing of South Dalton Control Stas	103
Computer generated drawings of South Dalton Zero Station Interior	102
Survey drawing of Rudston Out Stas	105
Survey drawing of Sigglesthorne Out Stas	109

Glossary of Abbreviations and Terms

AA	-	Anti Aircraft
ATS	-	Auxiliary Territorial Service
BAR	-	Browning Automatic Rifle
BEF	-	British Expeditionary Force
CIC	-	Commander in Chief
DCGS	-	Deputy Chief of the General Staff
GHQ	-	General Headquarters
GOC	-	General Officer Commanding
HE	-	High Explosives
HG	-	Home Guard
IO	-	Intelligence Officer
MI(R)	-	Military Intelligence (Research)
OB	-	Operational Base
OP	-	Observation Post
SAS	-	Special Air Service Regiment
SGW	-	Salt Glazed Ware
SMG	-	Submachine Gun

Intelligence Officer - The cover name for the commanding officer of an Auxiliary Unit Area, usually based on shire county boundaries.

Operational Base - The secret hide-out or base for an Auxiliary Unit patrol, normally providing accommodation and stores for up to seven men. In most cases they were constructed underground hence the generic term 'bunker' is often prescribed.

Observation Post - A one or two man, camouflaged, advanced viewing point, linked to the Operational Base by a hidden field telephone line. Generally at ground level, but a few were located in trees and other elevated positions.

Nissen Hut - A fabricated building of steel frame semi-circular sections clad with corrugated iron sheeting. Invented in 1915 by Colonel P.N. Nissen (a Canadian). A semi-circular OB is sometimes described as an ELEPHANT SHELTER, due to the use of 'Jumbo' type of corrugated iron.

Acknowledgements

Special thanks go to Reverend Peter Hollis (former Intelligence Officer, East Riding Auxiliary Units) and to former patrol members for providing much helpful information: -

Norman Blake (Beverley South Patrol), Frank Blanchard (Bewholme Patrol), George Boyes (Burton Fleming Patrol), David and Frank Byass (Bainton Patrol), Arthur Carr (Kilham Patrol), Arthur Clubley (Skirlaugh Patrol), George Conner (Withernsea Patrol), Dennis Cook (Westow Patrol), Ken Cooper (Burton Agnes Patrol), George Crawforth (Aldborough Patrol), John Elgey (Bainton Patrol), Norman Grise (Leavening Patrol), George Harrison (Lockington Patrol), Arthur Jackson (North Cave Patrol), Ed Maltby (Spaldington Patrol), Charlie Mason (South Cave Patrol), Harry Milson (Wharram Patrol), Eddie Shaw (Beverley South Patrol), Bill Smith (Beverley North Patrol), Duncan Suddaby (North Cave Patrol), Ben Taylor (South Cave Patrol), Claude Varley (Bewholme Patrol), John Woodcock (Bridlington North Patrol).

Mrs E M Cross, Harry Dixon, Brian Found, Mrs S Heathcote, Mrs Hodgson, Trevor and Clive Holley, Mrs M MacIntosh, Edward Moxlow Mrs Susan Pace, Mrs A Taylor and Mike Welton, all being relatives of former patrol members, provided much helpful information.

Former Special Duty Branch members, Arthur Gabbitas (Royal Signals), Stan Judd (Royal Signals) and Barbara Culleton (ex Junior Commander, ATS, Coleshill HQ) helped with the Intelligence radio network. Mrs Joy Chapel, whose late husband, Captain Kirk Chapel RE, built many of the wartime underground bases, provided information on some difficult site locations.

Thanks must also go to the many organisations, museums, landowners and individuals who over many years of research have contributed by providing information or giving access to their land and property: -

Dr William Ward, Mark Sansom, Alan Rudd, David Clarke, Roger Thomas, George Harwood, Sam Watson, Mark Bond, Mike Poole, George Dawes and Ian Sanderson (Defence of Britain Project volunteers). The Royal Engineers Museum, Chatham, and the Museum of British Resistance Organisation, Parham, in particular Andy Taylor and Colin Durrant. Keith Blaxhall. (Head Warden, Buscot and Coleshill Estate). Dave Evans & the Humber Archaeology Partnership

Arnold Atkinson, Tom Barnes, J & D Beachel, Jan Brooksbank, Peter Carver, Castle Hill Hospital, Martin Craven Colin Drew, John Dunning, Ernie Ellerington, Stuart Elliot, Mr Elvidge, Peter Emerton, Mr Fitzgerald, Brent Flint, Tessa Foote, Alan Gibson, Liz and Paul Gliddon, Mr Hamilton, Derrick Hasting, Mrs C Hobson, Andrew Horsley, The Lord Hotham, David Hutchinson, Raymond Ireland, Bernard Langton, Sir Charles Legard Bt, Sir Ian MacDonald of Sleat BT, Mrs J Mires, Mr & Mrs J Naylor, Rise Park Estate, Dawn Robinson, Jim Rocket, Martyn Taylor, Brenda Turner, Dave Wray.

The work of Simon Williamson in producing computer generated drawings of certain underground bunkers is greatly appreciated.

Finally, most grateful thanks to Christine Lancaster and Niki Mitchell, Westwood Office & Copy Services, for their long suffering in transcribing my hand written text, and also to Sandra Jessop for assistance with proof reading.

Over a long period of research many people have been interviewed and contributed towards the publication of this book. Many will have passed on, and if any names have been, inadvertently, omitted please accept my sincere apologies.

Issued by the Ministry of Information on behalf of the War Office and the Ministry of Home Security

STAY WHERE YOU ARE

IF this island is invaded by sea or air everyone who is not under orders must stay where he or she is. This is not simply advice: it is an order from the Government, and you must obey it just as soldiers obey their orders. Your order is "Stay Put", **but remember that this does not apply until invasion comes.**

Why must I stay put?

Because in France, Holland and Belgium, the Germans were helped by the people who took flight before them. Great crowds of refugees blocked all roads. The soldiers who could have defended them could not get at the enemy. The enemy used the refugees as a human shield. These refugees were got out on to the roads by rumour and false orders. Do not be caught out in this way. Do not take any notice of any story telling what the enemy has done or where he is. Do not take orders except from the Military, the Police, the Home Guard (L.D.V.) and the A.R.P. authorities or wardens.

What will happen to me if I don't stay put?

If you do not stay put you will stand a very good chance of being killed. The enemy may machine-gun you from the air in order to increase panic, or you may run into enemy forces which have landed behind you. An official German message was captured in Belgium which ran:

"Watch for civilian refugees on the roads. Harass them as much as possible."

Our soldiers will be hurrying to drive back the invader and will not be able to stop and help you. On the contrary, they will

1.1 Ministry of Information Leaflet, 1940. (Author's Collection)

1. Preface

In the summer of 1940, I queued with a group of Lincolnshire men to join the Home Guard. Their purpose was to help the Regular forces resist an imminent invasion by Nazi Germany.

On reaching the recruiting desk I requested my uniform and rifle. The reply was devastating! "Clear off little boy!" I was at least seven years old. They must of heard of Hitler Youth? Well, I considered myself and contemporaries as 'Churchill Youth'!

The only way out of this unexpected impasse was to form our very own private army. We drilled and carried out battle manoeuvres just like the Home Guard. We followed them everywhere, as they, being 'raw recruits' were guaranteed to drop some item of equipment!

At the time another civilian army was being secretly recruited around the British coast. It was over fifty years later that I first became aware of its wartime existence, and discovered that Charles Mason a fellow 'digger' from the East Riding Archaeological Society had been a former member of this most secret organisation in East Yorkshire.

Together, over a period of some seven years we have researched and recorded the activities of the East Yorkshire involvement within this mysterious army, as part of the National Defence of Britain Project.

In 1940 the Ministry of Information had issued a public information leaflet entitled 'STAY WHERE YOU ARE'. In the event of an enemy invasion the civilian population was ordered to 'stay-put', in order to avoid blocking roads and impeding movements of our own forces. In a strange way this order applied more so to this secret civilian army who unlike the Regular forces and Home Guard, were to remain behind with a more sinister agenda.

ALAN WILLIAMSON March 2003

2. Operation Sealion

During the summer of 1940 both sides of the English Channel were a hive of much activity, each side having an entirely opposite aim.

On the German occupied side all the ports were busy assembling a massive invasion force – destination England or more correctly named Operation Sealion. Some 1700 river and canal barges were being converted into troop and tank landing craft. A flotilla of merchant ships and tugs was also being assembled as were troop carrying planes of the Luftwaffe.

The invasion force planned to land on the south-east coast of England.

On the English side, the activity to resist an invasion was even more frantic, with little or no intelligence as to when or where the actual invasion would take place. Even East Anglia and the Wash areas were thought to be prime invasion locations, and in fact the whole east coast became subject to an Exclusion Order prohibiting unauthorised access within a 20 mile zone. A similar prohibition had existed during the First World War, which covered the whole of the British coastline.

Within this zone, apart from troop concentrations, hundreds of steel and concrete infantry and artillery positions, mainly small pillboxes were being erected to strengthen the actual beach defences of minefields and anti-tank obstructions.

All the roads leading from this 'coastal crust' as it became known, had road blocks and anti-tank ditches at strategic junctions. Additionally open fields and common land, suitable for the landing of troop carrying planes, including gliders, were either furrowed with ditches or had a grid of tall concrete posts linked with barbed wire.

Whilst Operation Dynamo had, miraculously, rescued 338,226 men, mainly of the British Expeditionary Force (BEF), from Dunkirk, left behind was virtually all of their equipment. This represented 2472 guns, 63,879 vehicles, 20,548 motorcycles 700 tanks and 500,000 tons of stores (i.e. ammunition). This short lived BEF campaign had also resulted in the loss of about 1000 aircraft.

In his now famous speech on the 4th June 1940 the Prime Minister, Winston Churchill said:

"We shall defend our island, whatever the cost may be. We shall fight on the beaches, we shall fight on the landing grounds, we shall fight in the fields and in the streets, we shall fight in the hills: we shall never surrender."

A fine stirring speech, but due to those massive equipment losses in France, and the lack of reserves, Great Britain at this stage possessed little weaponry to carry out the imminent fight.

There are varying reports as to the state of our armament at that stage. It has been suggested that there were only 176 anti-tank guns for the whole of the country and that the London Division, protecting the capital, had neither anti-tank guns nor Bren guns at that time. Most of our few remaining tanks were either lightly armoured or obsolete, incapable of putting up much of a fight against the German Panzer divisions. At the current production rate of tanks in June 1940, it would take 6-8 months for their replacement and a similar period for our field guns. This was at a critical time when the expected invasion was only days or weeks away.

The War Cabinet had approved a new strategy of defence which was to hold the enemy at their beachhead until our mobile reserve columns could man the inland specially prepared defences called STOPLINES. These were in reality gigantic anti-tank ditches, using where possible natural features such as canals and rivers. In other cases deep concrete ditches were created. The rivers Ouse and Trent formed the STOPLINE in Yorkshire.

Winston Churchill realised that our poorly equipped coastal defences would probably be unable to give our mobile reserve columns sufficient time to man the STOPLINES. Something else was needed to slow any enemy breakout from their coastal bridgeheads.

One answer was the creation of a highly secret volunteer army of saboteurs, called by the innocuous title 'AUXILIARY UNITS'.

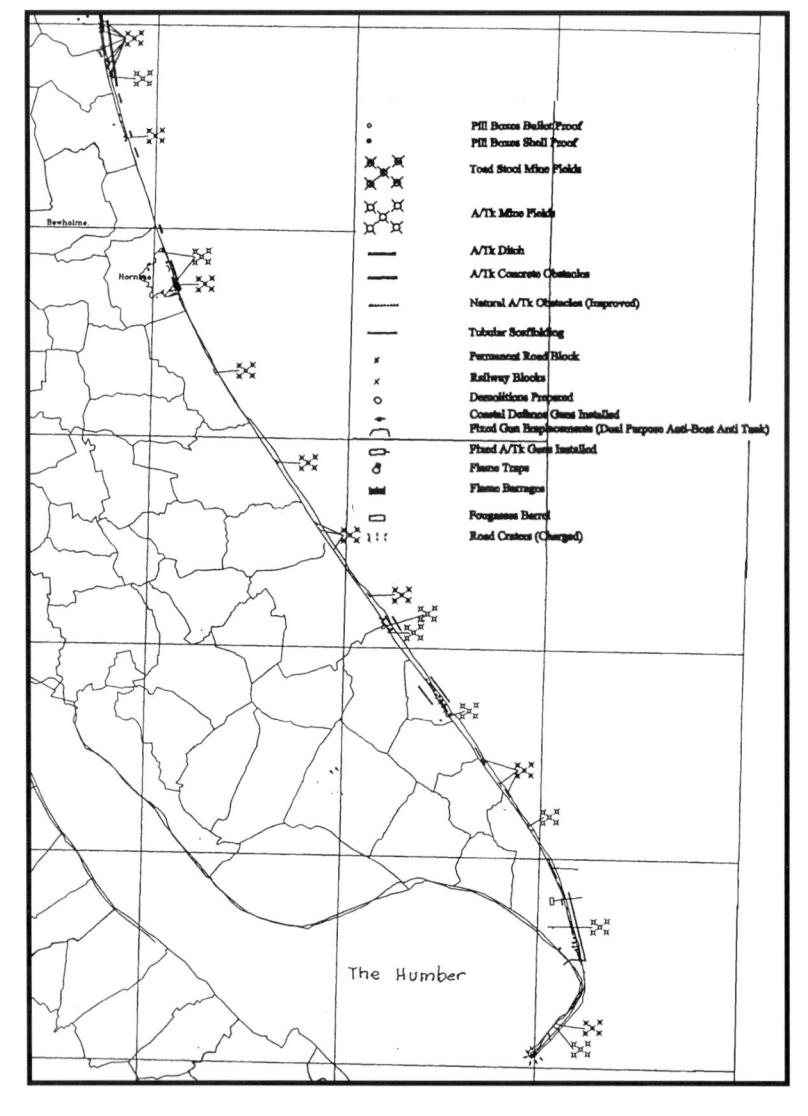

2.1 Coast Defence Plan, 1941, for the Holderness Coast Transcribed from an original military sketch plan. (Humber Archaeology Partnership)

3. Auxiliary Units

3.1 The Beginning

For some time, two government organisations, Section D of the Foreign Office, and M.I.(R) (Military Intelligence (Research)) had been exploring the then unthinkable possibility of an actual enemy invasion. Since 1939 a covert, but uncoordinated operation had attempted to recruit 'suitable' civilians who would be willing to form the embryo of a secret resistance group. This included the burying of the odd cache of ammunition/explosives for use in such an eventuality, and since the end of World War II, these well hidden, and obviously forgotten dumps, have made the occasional surprise re-appearance.

In fact the Hull Daily Mail, on the 6th April 1968, reported that a cache of explosives were found in a garden at Hornsea. Apparently the property owner, had been approached by a 'mystery man' in civilian clothing about the time of the Dunkirk operation. He was given petrol bombs, detonators/fuses etc and asked to form a resistance organisation should the Germans invade. Although he became a Home Guard officer he never became part of the Auxiliary Unit organisation.

With the evacuation of Dunkirk underway, the Authorities decided to formalise the recruitment of such a secret, civilian, resistance organisation. However this time it was to be under the aegis of the GHQ Home Forces (General Headquarters – Home Forces), whose Commander in Chief was Field Marshal Ironside.

The person chosen to establish this new 'secret army' was Colonel Colin Mcvean Gubbins, who had served with Field Marshal Ironside during the First World War Russian campaign.

Colonel Gubbins was ideally suited for this job, in that he had studied partisan operations in eastern Europe, and been sent to Poland in 1939 to organise a resistance movement should Germans invade Poland and Czechoslovakia. He had also produced pamphlets on guerrilla warfare, including one, on the subject of unarmed combat, aptly entitled 'Thuggery'. In early 1940, during the short-lived Norwegian campaign, Gubbins had successfully demonstrated the value of small independent and self-sufficient fighting units. These were later to become the basis of the new styled 'commando' units.

His new staff, initially based in Whitehall, was selected mostly from officers he had served with in Poland, France and Norway. Within one month he had established the first network of this secret army of civilian saboteurs.

A secret report by Colonel Gubbins dated 26 July 1940, to the CIC GHQ Home Forces, clearly sets out the aims, method of recruitment and progress of the Auxiliary Units. The main part of that report is set out below:-

S E C R E T.

AUXILIARY UNITS, HOME FORCES

A.   Organisation etc.

Object:

1. The object of Auxiliary Units, Home Forces, on the fighting side, is to build up, within the general body of the Home Guards, a series of small local units whose role is to act offensively on the flanks and in the rear of any German troops who may obtain a temporary foothold in this country.
The other role is Intelligence.

Method of Employment:

2. These Auxiliary Units are equipped with special Molotov bombs, delay action fuzes and plastic HE., incendiary bombs and devices of various kinds from non-military stocks, as well as the rifle and grenade. Their task is to harry and embarrass the enemy by all means in their power from the first day he lands, their particular targets being tanks and lorries in lager, ammunition dumps, HQs, small straggling parties and posts etc. Their object is, in co-operation with the regular forces, to prevent the invader establishing a secure foothold, and thus to facilitate his defeat.

3. These units must operate mainly by night and therefore are constituted entirely from local men who know their countryside intimately, i.e. farmers, game-keepers, hunt servants etc under a selected local leader. In certain areas where woodlands or heath are of considerable extent, particular units have the special role of occupying prepared 'hide-outs' as a base for operations. These hide-outs are being prepared and provided with reserve stocks of food, water, munitions of various kinds etc., so as to extend the period during which operations can be carried on.

4. In all cases, the organisation and operations of these Auxiliary Units are being planned in the closest co-operation with the local Commander, either Corps, Division, or Area, and with Home Guard Area Commander, to ensure that their action shall be effective, and in conformity with the military plan. At the same time, in order to ensure the necessary degree of secrecy, the sites of the dumps of special stores for these units are not disclosed except to the local leader, and the units are given the general title of 'Observation Units' to mask their real role. Secrecy beyond this degree would merely handicap efficiency.

On the 8th August 1940, based on the Colonel Gubbins report, Duncan Sandys, War Cabinet Secretary, wrote to the Prime Minister to inform him as to the progress of the Auxiliary Units. He concluded by stating that:-

"From the above you will see that these Auxiliary Units, although only very recently formed, are going rapidly ahead, and shall soon be in a position to give valuable help to the regular forces.

I think you will agree that they are doing well and deserve encouragement. With your permission, therefore, I would like to tell Home Forces that you attach importance to the work of this branch of the Home Guard and are pleased with the progress made."

This new 'secret army' clearly had the full backing of the Prime Minister who wrote to the Secretary of State for War in September 1940, stating that

"I have been following with much interest the growth and development of the new guerrilla formations ... known as 'Auxiliary Units'. From what I hear these units are being organised with thoroughness and imagination, and should, in the event of invasion, prove a useful addition to the regular forces. Perhaps you will keep me informed of progress."

3.2 Recruitment

The most obvious invasion coasts were those nearest to the Continent, being Kent, Sussex and East Anglia. The first Intelligence Officers (IOs) sent there to start recruiting were Peter Fleming, author brother of 'James Bond' creator, Ian Fleming, and Andrew Thorne, the well known Arctic Explorer.

By 1942 the whole of the British coastline from Caithness, Scotland, around the southern English coast to Pembroke, South Wales had a network of some twenty Auxiliary Unit operational areas. These were generally based on existing county boundaries, and each under the control of an IO. The IOs were mostly volunteer regular forces officers with the rank of Captain, and their cover name of Intelligence Officers only contact with the normal Intelligence Corps was in respect of 'pay and rations'.

It was a distinct advantage if the IO either came from, or was familiar with, the area he commanded, both in establishing the areas for specific patrols and recruiting local leaders. Many of the patrol leaders would be recruited from the Home Guard on the recommendation of their appropriate senior commander. Naturally the best, and most fit men were selected, often much to the annoyance of the local Home Guard officer, who would be kept strictly unaware of their secret function. The true nature of the organisation was known only to the upper echelon of the regular forces, and even then only a broad picture.

The local police would be involved only in giving a character assessment of recruits. The typical patrol leader would often be a farmer or gamekeeper, preferably with military experience, such as World War I veterans.

The patrol leader would then recruit the other men for his 7-man group. Invariably they would be well known to each other and with similar employment. Although they were required to sign the Official Secrets Act, they were not enrolled in either the regular forces or Home Guard. They were in effect private citizens, who if caught during their guerrilla activities, would not have the protection of the Geneva Convention and were more than likely to be shot.

The fact that they were in Home Guard uniform and indeed some had been transferred from their local battalion, proved to be an excellent cover story. Today, for this very reason, it is difficult to research the organisation as the public still retain the perception that they were all in the Home Guard. Their true identity was also kept from their families.

Eventually some 640 + patrols had been formed with a total force 4200 men. At a later date, a number of patrols would be grouped together, with one of the patrol leaders being commissioned as a Group Leader.

3.3 Operational Bases

To fulfil their role as stay behind guerrilla units, patrols needed a hide-out, initially in order to go to ground as the invader would approach, and thereafter from where to conduct their operations. As the word 'hide-out' was a little too obvious as to their true nature, it was subsequently changed to 'operational base' (OB).

In the initial rush to meet the imminent invasion literally any hole in the ground, including caves and cellars, were utilised. A simple square dugout, varying in size from 8ft (2.4m) to 12ft (3.6m) was often used. Usually the floor level below ground would be 8-10ft (2.4-3.0m) with internal height of 6-7ft (1.8-2.1m). The roof would be covered with whatever materials were readily available, i.e. flat corrugated steel sheets or layers of chicken wire, carried on wooden posts. This in turn would be covered with sufficient soil to provide a vegetation cover. The entrance would be direct into the dugout via a wooden hatch and steps. The ventilation was primitive and often through a hole in the roof. These early dugouts could be referred to as MkIs, and were constructed by either regular engineer/pioneer units or the patrols themselves.

However, not all OBs were built entirely by army personnel. David Clark, a retired Scunthorpe builder, recalls John Sheffield Constructional Co., a local firm, being contracted to assist in the building of all the Lincolnshire OBs, right from the Humber down to Deeping St James. At the time he was responsible for all the brickwork, the other less specialist work being carried out by regular army troops from the Leicestershire Regiment. Each OB took them about 2 weeks to construct, working from 8.00 am until 5.00 pm each day.

With the immediate threat of invasion being postponed, the military gave serious thought to the proper construction of OBs and their location. In 1941 the Royal Engineers produced a standard drawing for the construction of OBs, which, could be modified to suit the location. It is titled 'Auxiliary Unit shelter' and could be referred to as the MkII version. This was basically a small 'Nissen' type hut constructed of curved heavy gauge, corrugated steel with the ends sealed by 9" (0.2m) solid brick walls. The standard version shows measurements of 22'.9"(6.9m) long 9'.6"(2.9m) wide and 7' (2.1m) high.

Unlike the carlier MkI types, the standard drawing shows an escape tunnel and exit hatch, described as a 'bolt-hole'. To the majority of the surviving patrol members this is commonly referred to as an 'escape' although in one case it was shown on a construction drawing as an 'exit creep'.

Ventilation, in those days, was not an exact science- more trial and error with the patrol members as guinea pigs! Many tales exist of unconscious men being dragged out in the nick of time. Salt glazedware pipes of either 3" or 6" diameter were the standard ventilation pipes built into the end wall, incoming air being brought in via floor level pipes and foul air extracted by high level pipes. Another system used was a 'manifold' of 4 separate pipes at 90° to each other, cut into the roof centre, thereby using the various directions of the wind for extraction purposes. In one or two cases they appear to be after thoughts to remedy a failing system, and have proved to be a later weakness to the integrity of the structure. The ends of these pipes surfaced either in hollowed out tree trunks or disguised as rabbit holes, but covered with chicken wire mesh to prevent the entry of such wildlife.

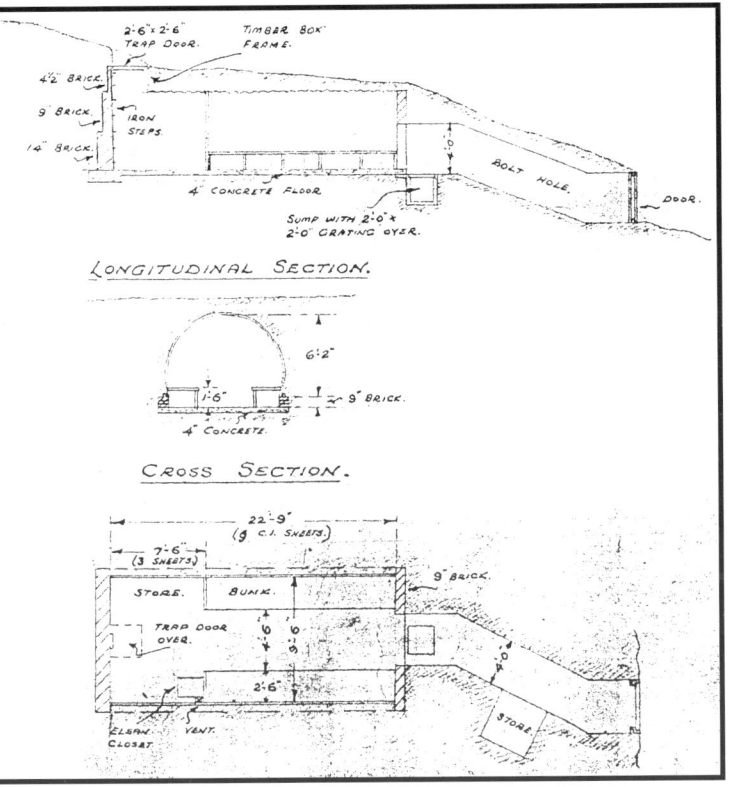

3.1 H Q Staff and Intelligence Officers, Coleshill House, Feb 1941. (Miss E M Wilmot coll.)

3.2 1941 Construction Drawing of an Auxiliary Unit Shelter (OB) (MkII). (Public Record Office)

The entrance and exits were through the end brick walls, covered by hinged or sliding doors. The actual surface entry and escape hatches were camouflaged, sometimes consisting of a wooden tray containing vegetation and concealed by a sliding, cantilevered special hollow tree trunk. The escape tunnels were usually 3-4ft (0.9-1.2m) square, the sides being revetted with flat corrugated steel sheets and wooden posts. The roof would again be flat corrugated sheets laid on salvaged timber posts or angle iron.

The floors were either poured concrete or concrete pavers. A later version of the standard OB had extra baffle walls at both ends, which formed small 2.6" (0.76m) wide vestibules, giving extra protection to those within the main chamber or escaping. A hand grenade dropped down the entry hatch, without the baffle wall, would have wiped out the entire patrol. These vestibule areas became very handy for storage and toilet purposes. This later version, invariably using concrete blocks instead of bricks, can be referred to as a MkIII type. Other variations to the standard pattern occur, due to the particularly difficult locations, such as land with a high water table. OBs in the low lying areas, in the Kent marshes and the East coast, were sometimes constructed as a waterproofed reinforced concrete tank with a flat concrete roof.

OB Equipment

Within the OB there would be four wooden bunks and possibly a folding table. Lighting was provided by paraffin Tilley lamps and candles. Heating and cooking was done with Primus stoves. Fragments of cast iron stoves have been found near OBs suggesting that these could be used for heating purposes as many of the basic structures, on being handed over to the patrols, were then 'customised' with most elaborate features.

Toilet facilities were provided by an Elsan chemical closet. In addition to composite ration food packs and paraffin tanks, water was provided from an outside concealed tank piped to a tap in the main chamber. A one gallon jar of rum was also provided for 'emergency' purposes. Many an ingenious method was used for removing the rum, and replacing it with cold tea without removing the cork seal. A cattle hypodermic syringe was one of the recommended methods!

A limited amount of ammunition and explosives would be kept with the OB' but for safety reasons not within the main chamber. Separate, nearby, buried stores were considered a safer option, and that meant, if the OB was captured, not all the equipment would be lost.

Each OB was provided with 2 field telephones, one of which would be hidden in a nearby Observation Post (OP) and linked to the OB via a buried cable. The OP would be a 1 or 2 man size, camouflaged foxhole, located in a strategic position from where to observe enemy troop movements, and to provide an early warning system should the OB be approached. It would also provide a point of contact for neighbouring patrols.

Not all OPs would be constructed partially underground, sometimes trees and derelict buildings would be utilised.

OB Location

The basic principle was that all OBs should located within a 20-30 mile (32-48 km) coastal belt, some actually being within a mile of the sea. However, more recent discoveries have revealed the existence of a small number of patrols, much further inland, protecting the south-western approaches to the Black Country industrial heartland.

The siting of each OB appears to have been the decision of the IO in consultation with the appropriate patrol leader. A study of locations suggest that a key factor was the proximity of a possible strategic target or targets i.e. airfields, barracks, railway bridges/tunnels, and large country houses suitable for enemy headquarters.

One perceived danger in the early part of the War, was that the German Forces, using airborne troops, could capture an airfield near a vulnerable British port. It would then enable heavy armour and other equipment to be landed by sea. As a result, a report by General Taylor, Inspector General of Fortification in September 1940 (the Taylor Report on Ground Defence of Aerodromes) recommended that all airfields within 20 miles of a vulnerable port (Hull and Bridlington were specified) should be made Class I airfields for the purpose of ground defence purposes. This in effect strengthened ground defence in terms of strong points, weaponry and manpower.

In the East Riding, Brough, Catfoss, Driffield, Leconfield and Cottam were listed as Class I airfields, and this, obviously, accounts for many OBs sited in close proximity. It is recorded that penetration of airfields, and resultant sabotage, was a high priority in many patrol's training programme.

The early locations of some MkI OBs were dangerously close to important road junctions which would have been the subject of a substantial enemy presence, thus severely curtailing any unobtrusive operations from the OBs. However, some being in excellent locations, although unsuitable for the main OB, were retained as annexes and used for ammunition/explosives stores.

One other important factor was the need to reach a remote OB without leaving obvious trails in the vegetation. The near proximity of a little used public footpath or hedgerow became the answer to this problem. In any event most of the training was carried out well away from OBs which prevented the constant trampling of the undergrowth.

Where possible they were sited in woodland or near mature hedgerows to prevent enemy surveillance from the air. Even during construction, camouflage nets were used to hide the operation, and "alleged enemy bombing raids" or mortar bomb training excises used to explain the noise of explosive charges involved in blasting the large cavities required.

The sites of old quarries were other popular locations, enabling a rapid concealed emergency exit down to the quarry bottom. The speed of uncontrollable descent from one such quarry side escape hatch is an experience not easily forgotten! The author did it!

Whilst all OBs were provided with a small water tank, the presence of streams and springs was another factor in their location. It will be noticed that the standard equipment list for OBs included water sterilisation packs. Most OBs contained a sump for drainage purposes, but again, nearby rivers and ditches would have been useful.

In low lying areas, without the benefit of woodland and hedgerows, OBs were commonly built into the sides of deep ditches and drains. This again provided cover of movement both for gaining access to the OB but also for patrol operations. On other occasions a remote derelict building such as a windmill tower or farm building, would be a useful location in providing both access to an underground, cellar type OB, and an elevated OP.

Operational Bases for Intelligence Officers

Whilst all the patrols had an OB to operate from should an invasion occur, no similar provision had been made for IOs.

Some local army commanders had the idea that I.Os would immediately join their own HQ, and expect them to make dangerous journeys through enemy lines to contact their patrols.

In views of the seriousness of this problem Lt. Col. Beyts (Aux. Unit HQ) produced a report for Major General Gregson-Ellis (DCGS, FHQ, Home Forces) dated 21 May 1942 to justify I.Os having their own OB. Two of the major factors set out were :-

"
1.   In all guerrilla warfare there must be a leader. The I.O of each area is recognised by his patrols as such. The moral effect of knowing that their leader is sharing their dangers and in their midst is unquestionably more stimulating than the knowledge that he is installed on the British side of the line, directing them, or perchance misdirecting them, from a safe distance.
2.   The ability to convey orders for patrols to act on a Divisional or Corps Commander's instructions depends entirely on the I.O. being able to get through the enemy to the patrol which will have to carry out the order. The I.O may be lucky once, but the chances are that his G.O.C will never see him again."

The report suggested that the provision of nineteen OBs for IOs would cost, using military labour, a total of £2,000. It is presumed that this report was agreed, as evidence today reveals the existence of such OBs. Those found are much larger and better equipped than the standard patrol OB. Being constructed at this later date, they obviously avoided all weaknesses found in the early patrol OBs. They needed larger storage areas from which to re-supply the patrols and also to accommodate additional men should a patrol be unable to use their own base. Having since shown some former patrol members photographs and drawings of these 'Hilton Hotel' type OBs, their immediate reaction was of total envy!

A request was also made that IOs should have their own special portable radio set, to enable them to communicate with the British side of the line. The particular set in question No 17 R/T, was contained in a special reinforced cardboard case measuring approx. 18" x 12" x 6".

3.6 Cast iron gatepost cap used as counterweight for OB hatch cover. Note the staple embedded base for attaching rope/wire. (Author)

3.4 Equipment

Whilst the Home Guard, and to some extent the regular forces, were short of weapons and ammunition, the Auxiliary Units were very well equipped with weaponry and the most up to date sabotage materials. In particular, they had the latest time-delayed action fuses known as 'time-pencils' due to their size and shape. The prototype of this had been brought back from Poland by Col. Gubbins on his escape from the advancing enemy in 1939.

One immediate piece of identification is that all ranks carried personal side arms e.g. revolvers and similar automatic hand guns. The Prime Minister had personally intervened to ensure that they had these weapons. Rumours abound that they, together with the Tommy gun (Thompson Sub-machine Gun) were the confiscated property of gangsters in the USA. It is a known fact that these guns were obtained from that country.

Each patrol was issued with two .300 rifles, (Canadian Ross), and one .22 sniper rifle fitted with telescopic sights and a silencer. Prior to the 'Tommy Gun', they were also issued with the American .30 Browning Automatic Rifle (BAR), the standard USA Infantry weapon in World War II. This, like the Tommy Gun was too heavy for covert operations, and was replaced in late 1941 by the British 9mm Sten Gun. This was the most outstanding weapon of World War II and became the standard weapon supplied to resistance groups throughout occupied Europe. Its weight and size made it eminently suitable for the Auxiliary Units. Some later models were fitted with a silencer.

The other most important weapon issued was the fighting knife, which could be strapped, in its sheaf, to either leg or arm. The original was designed and made in the Shanghai Police Armoury in 1931 by two British Officers, W.E. Fairbairn and E.A. Sykes. It was produced in quantity in 1941, by the Wilkinson Sword Co, to become the standard fighting knife for our special forces.

The following list of special equipment for Auxiliary patrols appears to have been issued about 1940/41 prior to the introduction of the Sten Gun. The list is in addition to personal items of uniform clothing e.g. battle dress, denim overalls, greatcoat, leather boots etc, issued as standard to Regular Forces and the Home Guard.

MOST SECRET

List of Arms, Ammunition, Stores and Equipment required for the Patrol, Auxunits.

1. ARMS
7 Revolvers .38 American
2 Rifles .300
7 knives fighting
3 knobkerries
48 Grenades, 36M.4 sec.
3 Cases S.T. Grenades
2 Cases A.W. bottles
1 Rifle .22 with Silencer
1 Thompson Sub Machine Gun

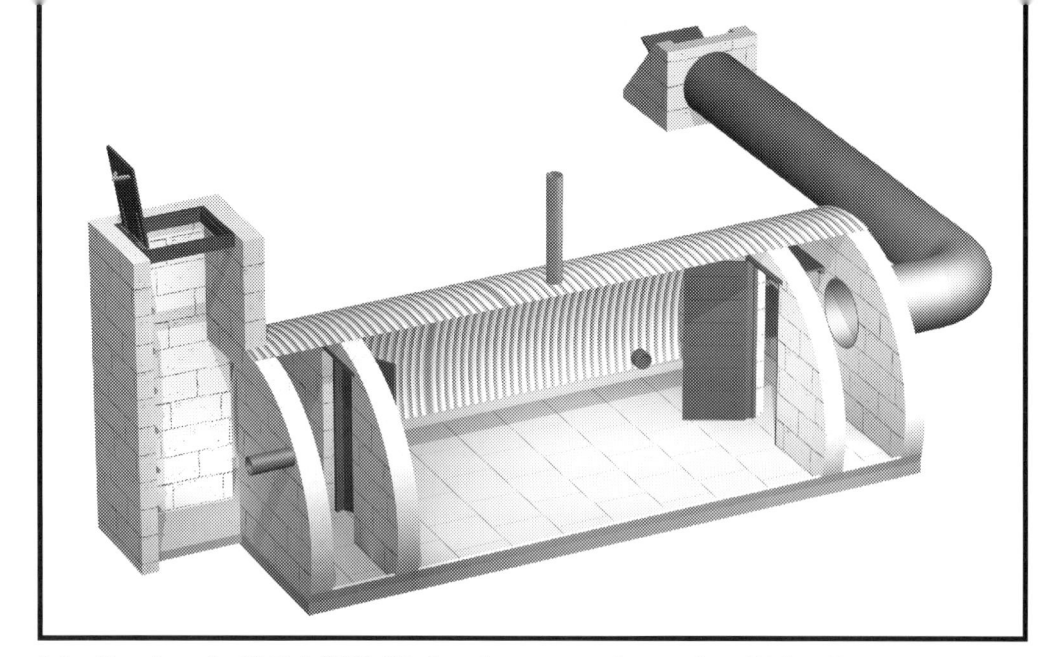

3.3 Drawing of a 1942 (MkIII) OB, based on an actual example at Bishop Burton. (Simon Williamson. Copyright)

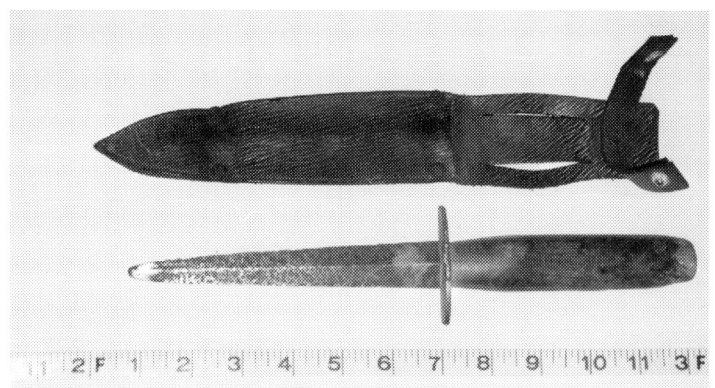

3.4 "Swords to Ploughshares" – Charlie Mason's original wartime commando knife, now used for peaceful garden weeding purposes. (Author)

3.5 Some of Charlie Mason's original equipment: rubber boots, wire cutters and magnets for attaching demolition charges to armoured vehicles etc. (Author)

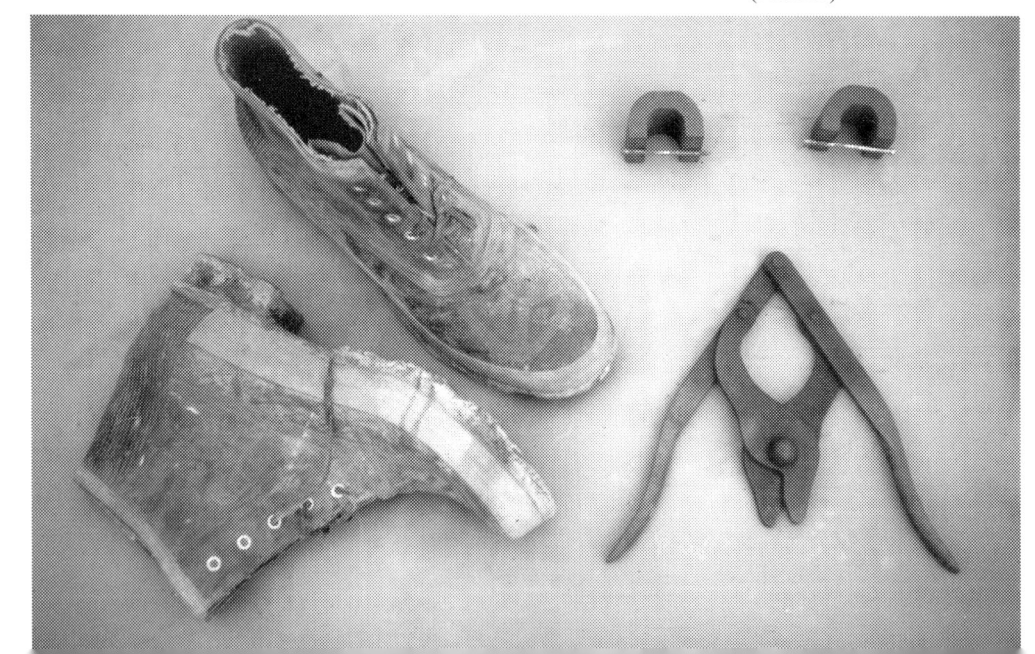

2. EXPLOSIVES
4 Auxunits (boxes containing explosives and concomitants)

3. AMMUNITION
40 rds .38 American
200 rds. .300
1000 rds .45 for S.M.G.
200 rds .22

4. EQUIPMENT
7 Holsters (Leather American)
7 Groundsheets
7 Blankets
7 Pairs Rubber boots (Agricultural workers type)
7 Water bottles, carriers and slings
1 set of equipment Thompson Sub Machine Gun
1 pair or wire cutters
1 Monocular and case

5. ELEPHANT SHELTER
The provision of one Elephant Shelter for construction work. The necessary equipment for furnishing the base, i.e. one Tilley Lamp, two Primus Stoves, Elsan chemical closet.

6. INTERCOMMUNICATION
One pair telephone DV
½ mile American cable, Type E

7. RATIONS
7 Composite Packs
1 Gallon Rum
10 Gallons Paraffin

8. MEDICAL STORES
1 First Aid Set (with morphia)
7 Water sterilisation sets
3 Shell dressings

At local level, this list of standard equipment would vary, sometimes being added to by customised weapons such as the 'wire garrote', said by some patrol members to be a much quieter and cleaner method of killing.

Item 2, Explosives, refers to the box of explosives, fuses, fuse wires etc required for their principal operation of sabotage. A detailed list of the contents of one such box is set out below. However, this list, dated July 1944, may well indicate material, and quantity, not available in the earlier days.

Appendix "A" to HF/3246/Q dated   Jul 44

Contents of One Aux. Unit Mark II

24 Copper Tube Igniters
6 Striker Boards
12 Pocket Tins Incendiaries (either Red, White or green markings)
20 1-hr Lead Delays
50 3-hr Lead Delays

50' Instantanious Fuze (Orange Line)
240 ft Cordtax
100 Detonators (Nos. 8 or 27)
20 lbs. Explosive. (Nobels 808, Polar Gelignite or Plastic)
48 ft Safety Fuze Mk II Bickford
20 C.E. Primers (Two Tins of 10 each)
24 Tubes, Fuze, Sealing, in those Aux. Units where the fuze is not packed in tins.
1 Crimping Tool
1 Tube Vaseline
1 Spool Trip Wire .032"
3 Spools Trap Wire .014"
8 Coils Tape
1 Sandbag
6 Pull Switches
3 Pressure Switches

Notes
1. Aux. Units Mark II held in the Northumberland Area may be deficient of Copper Tube Igniters.
2. A large number of Aux. Units Mark II will be defective of 3-hr L.Delays. Exact details are not obtainable but of the 360,00 which should be in circulation only 107,000 are actually contained in the Aux. Units enumerated in Appendix "B"
3. A large proportion of the Aux. Units Mark II will contain Magnets either Large or Small type. The number of these in each Aux. Unit will be about 6.

3.5 Training

In August 1940, Colehill House, in Berkshire, became the training headquarters for the Auxiliary Units. This was an ideal location, set in a small estate village surrounded by ample park and woodland. Remote from prying eyes but close enough to nearby Swindon for communication purposes.

Both the main house and the extensive courtyard stable block, provided adequate sleeping and office accommodation.

Eventually the main Auxiliary Unit HQ, having suffered considerable bomb damage at its Whitehall location also moved to Coleshill.

Every weekend a batch of Auxiliary Unit patrol members would report for intensive training. Initially, they were required to report to the Post Office, in the nearby small town of Highworth. The local postmistress, Mrs Mabel Stranks, would 'vet' the men, and if satisfied as to their identity, telephone Coleshill Hall for their collection by military transport.

This Post Office was not just used as a collection point, as all official correspondence had the Auxiliary Unit HQ address as *"c/o G.P.O Highworth, Nr Swindon, Wilts"*.

The training sessions would last from Friday until Sunday, and provide the patrol members *"with what every good guerrilla should know"*.

Training was given in unarmed combat, explosives, weaponry and guerrilla tactics. These newly acquired skills would then be tested in night time exercises.

In addition to the standard military training manuals, a number of specialised pamphlets were specially produced for the Auxiliary Units, including one entitled 'Thuggery', a most apt name for unarmed combat! Three of the printed pamphlets had rather interesting cover titles describing themselves as 'Calendar 1937', Calendar 1938' and the 'Countryman's Diary 1939'.

These innocuously titled covers contained detailed information on explosives, bombs and booby traps, and their most effective use on enemy supply dumps, static aircraft and armoured vehicles etc. It is thought that these were written between 1940 and 1943, and that had they been inadvertently left lying around, their description as out of date calendars and diaries would have prevented further examination.

The HQ training team comprised specialists in many disciplines, including regular commando type detachments described as Scout Patrols. In many cases these Scout Patrols were attached to an individual Auxiliary Unit area providing training back-up for the local Intelligence Officer. Later more and more training was carried out on a regional and local basis thus resulting in the saving of manpower and travelling costs.

Training at Coleshill was in addition to the local training at Patrol and Group level, which in the early days was most intensive, with the men being required to give at least twice the commitment of the standard Home Guard. Army drill and parades were the least of their concerns in 1940/41. However crawling through dense undergrowth at night covered in mud was important. Even in 1944 some patrols were training at least three nights a week.

3.7 Training programme for 15-17 August 1941 at Coleshill HQ. (Author's coll.)

PROGRAMME FOR WEEKEND 15TH-17TH AUGUST, 1941

DAY	SYNDI-CATE	0830-0925	0930-1025	1030-1125	1130-1225	1245-1345	1400-1600	1615-1800	1830-1930	1930-2030	2100-2330			
FRIDAY								Course Assembles		Dinner 2000 hrs	Opening address by Colonel Major followed by lecture on Intercommunication by Major Beyts			
						1350-1450	1500-1630	1630-1650	1700-1800	1800-1900	1910-2000	2000-2100	2130-2300
SATUR-DAY	A	Lecture on Ex-plosives	Ex-plosives	Revolver	Mills Bomb	LUNCH	Un-armed Combat	Patrol lecture	Tea at Ambush site	Recce for Patrol	Lecture on Guerrilla tactics in the recent Abyssinian campaign	DINNER	Lecture on German Army	Night Patrol
	B		Revolver	Mills Bomb	Ex-plosives									
	C		Mills Bomb	Ex-plosives	Revolver									
		0900-0955	1000-1035	1100-1155	1200-1230	1245-1300	1345							
SUNDAY	A	Bases	Tommy Gun Mech-ansim	Ex-plosives	Farewell Address by Colonel Major	Tommy Gun Firing	LUNCH (After which course dis-perses)							
	B	Tommy Gun Mech-anism	Ex-plosives	Bases										
	C	Ex-plosives	Bases	Tommy Gun Mech-anism										

12th August, 1941

3.8 Surviving Palladian style gate pillars at Coleshill House. The former house was designed by Sir Roger Pratt, in consultation with Inigo Jones and was demolished in 1952 following a fire. (Author 2000)

3.9 The surviving stable block at Coleshill was formerly used by the Auxiliary Units for HQ offices and accommodation. (Author 2000)

3.10 The former Post Office at Highworth, which was the official address for the Auxiliary Units HQ at Coleshill House. (Author 2000)

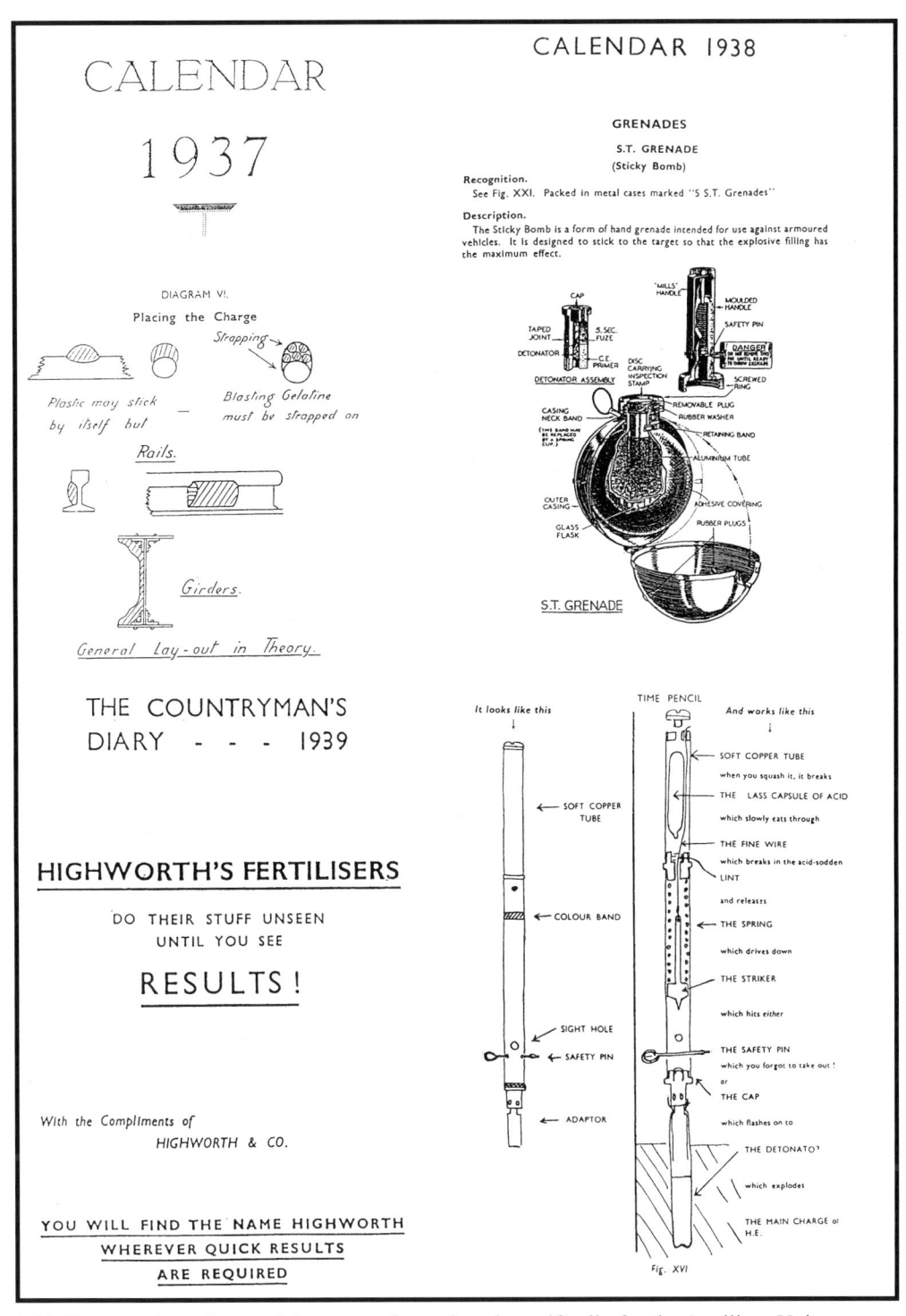

3.11 Extracts from three training manuals produced specifically for the Auxiliary Units. (Author's coll.)

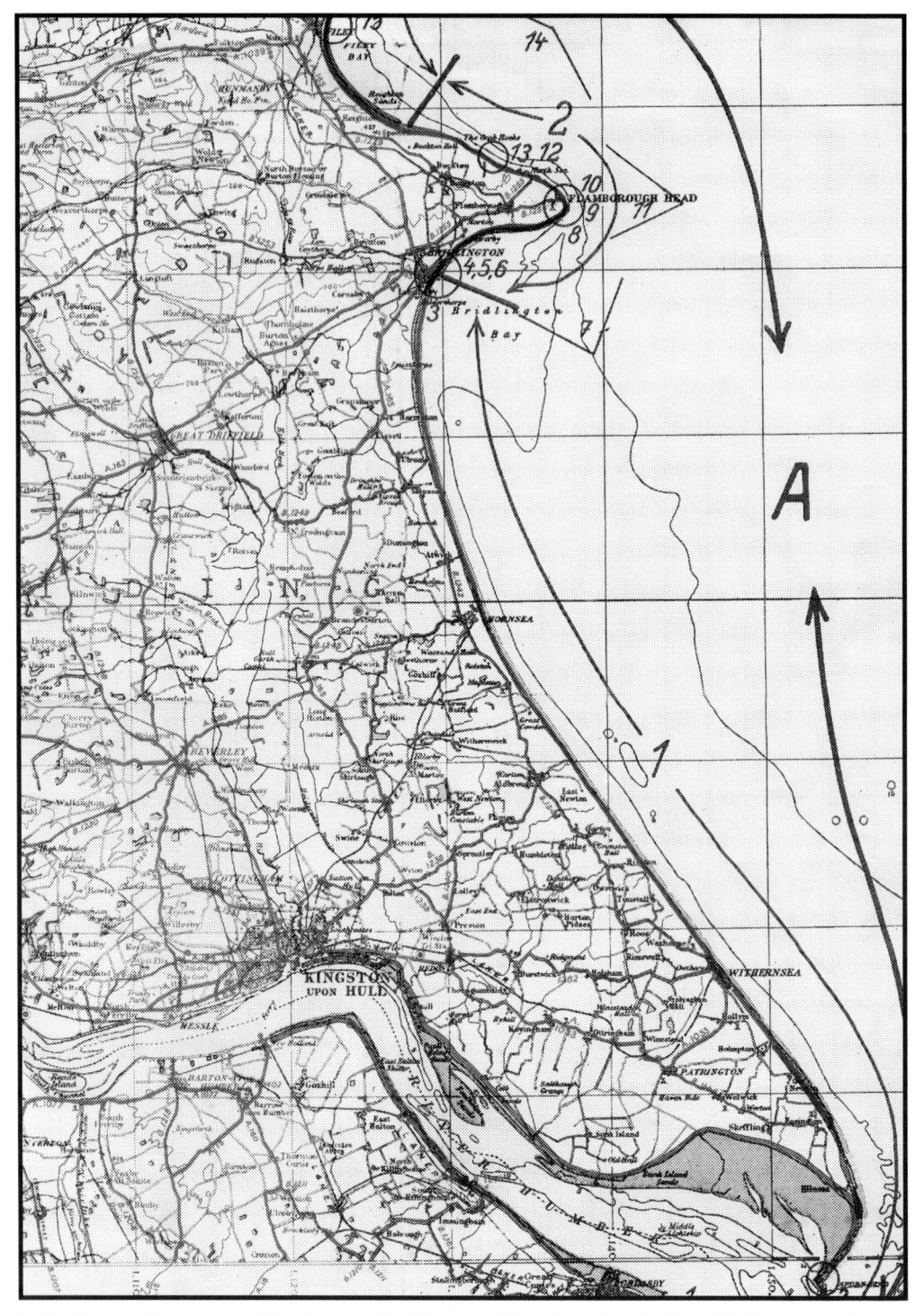

3.12 Extract from the 1940s German Intelligence Map showing the East Riding coastal area. (Metcalfe Collection University of Hull)

4. East Riding Auxiliary Units

In the preliminary days of invasion planning, the German High Command had given consideration to landings on the East Coast between the Thames and Newcastle. German Naval Intelligence had prepared reports on landing beaches and coastal defences between the Wash and Flamborough. Documents captured during the later Allied advance into Germany revealed detailed studies of the East Coast entitled "Militargeographische Einzelangalsen über Nordost-England" (Military Geographic Targets in North East England). This combination of photographs plus geological and road maps referred to the nature of beaches, defences and other important installations. Similar reports were prepared for other potential landing areas. They are dated between 1940 and 1942. The Humber and the East Yorkshire coast figure prominently in these documents.

Even when the decision to invade along the channel coast had been taken, the Operation Section included plans for a false diversionary attack to be made on the East coast, code named 'Herbstreise', to give the Allies the impression that this was the main landing area with the Channel coast landings being a minor diversionary attack.

There had in fact been an earlier diversionary plan to land two infantry divisions north of the Humber. Therefore the British military planners had to take all these possible options quite seriously, hence the heavy coastal crust of anti-invasion defences lining the East Yorkshire coast and the Humber.

Like other County structures, the East Riding patrols did not happen overnight, but were built up over a period of months, possibly even a year.

The creation of a resistance unit was not entirely new to the East Riding. During the first Napoleonic invasion scare, Lt General Scott gave orders, in March 1797 to the Commanding Officer of the company quartered at Patrington in the event of invasion. Until re-inforcements could arrive the Orders stated "*it may be expected that the Farmers and Peasantry will turn out in defence of their property and that those who may not be employed in driving the cattle or on other duties that will be pointed out to them in due time will join the military and assist materially in harassing him on his march by getting on his flanks, provided that can be done under cover in the more enclosed parts of the country, it not being either expected or deserved that any men should expose themselves further than it may be in their power to harass and alarm the enemy if advancing and as all approaches to the road that the enemy may take must be perfectly known to all the people who live near it and who may be of use in checking the enemies progress, without any great danger to themselves small parties and even single men will easily know when to place themselves to advantage...*"

This order specifies precisely the role and make up of the Auxiliary Units, 143 years later, in that in the event of an invasion from the continent, local farmers with a detailed knowledge of their countryside, working from cover in small groups, would be required to carry out delaying tactics pending the arrival of regular re-inforcements

The first person to be recruited was the Commanding Officer or Intelligence Officer (IO). In this case the person in question was Peter Hollis, the son of Canon Hollis, the then vicar of Hornsea. Peter Hollis had enlisted in the Territorial Army (E. Yorkshire Regiment) in September 1939 at the age of 19. He was commissioned as a 2nd Lieutenant in May 1940, and following the Dunkirk operation, volunteered for this, previously unknown, role as an Intelligence Officer with the Auxiliary Units. He was an ideal person for the position, having been born in Hull and educated at Pocklington School, he had a good knowledge of the county geography, essential to establishing Auxiliary Unit patrols in strategic locations.

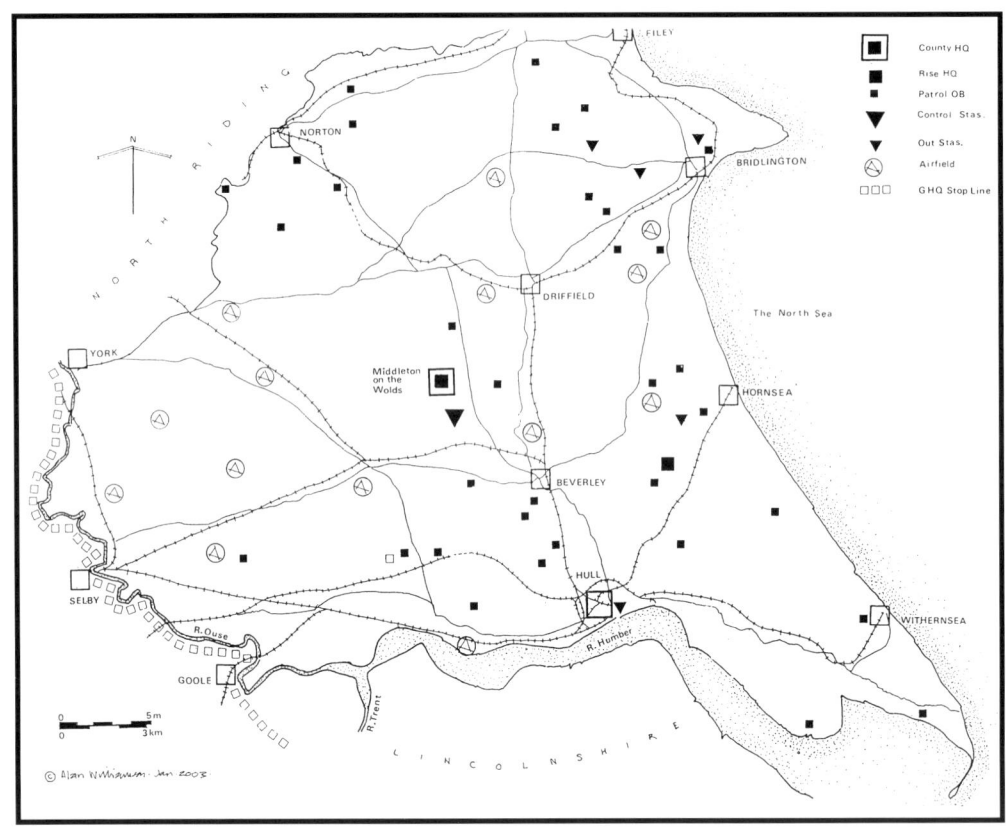

4.1 The location of various East Riding Auxiliary Unit bases. The outline map shows pre-war major roads and railways. (Author)

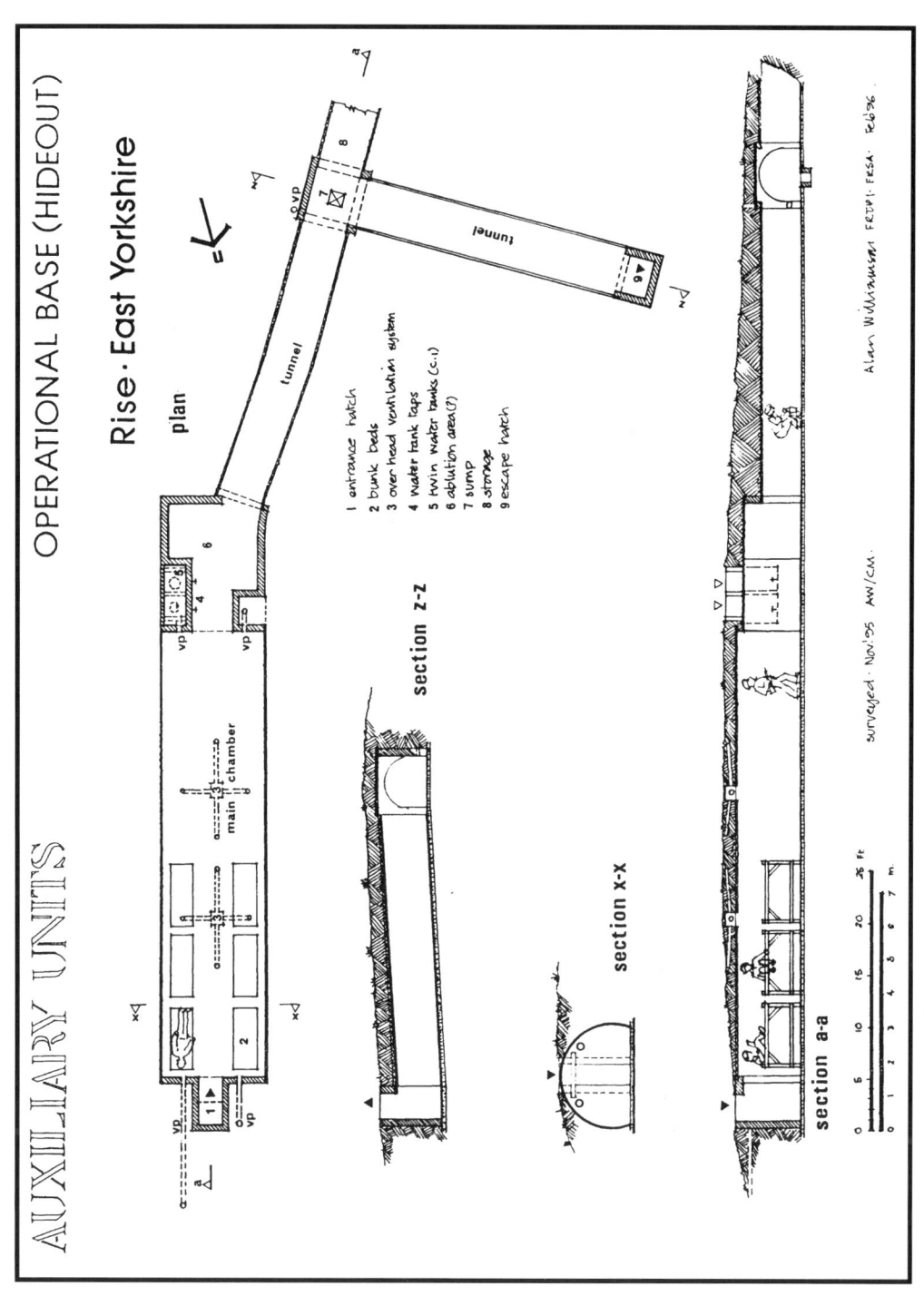

4.2 Survey drawing of the Rise OB in 1995. (Author)

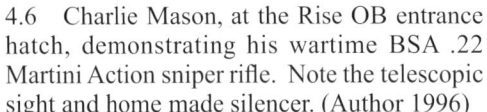

4.3   Two water taps (both cold!) inside the Rise OB. Note white paint around each tap to aid location in semidarkness. (Author)

4.4   Charlie Mason with remains of the surviving bunk beds inside the Rise OB. (Author 1995)

4.5   Lieutenant Peter Hollis (later Captain) newly commissioned into the East Yorkshire regiment in 1940. (Rev Peter Hollis)

4.6   Charlie Mason, at the Rise OB entrance hatch, demonstrating his wartime BSA .22 Martini Action sniper rifle. Note the telescopic sight and home made silencer. (Author 1996)

4.7 Charlie Mason at the entrance to the Middleton HQ OB. Note the rope ladder, specially manufactured for 'bunker' surveys. (Author 1996)

4.8 Interior view of entrance chamber, Middleton HQ OB. The candles are not for any pagan rites, purely to provide excellent general lighting for survey purposes! (Author 1996)

4.9 The Crown and Anchor P.H. at Middleton on the Wolds. This was the popular, unofficial HQ of the East Riding Auxiliary Units. (Author 2002)

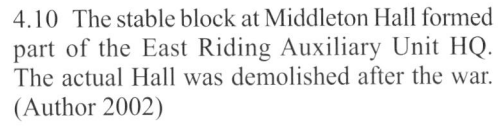

4.10 The stable block at Middleton Hall formed part of the East Riding Auxiliary Unit HQ. The actual Hall was demolished after the war. (Author 2002)

His first job was to interview suitable candidates for the role of patrol leaders, and have their background vetted by the local police. He had a small cadre of Regular soldiers to assist him in the training of his 'new army'. His first HQ was Beningholme Hall, near Skirlaugh. This HQ was later moved to Rise Hall, which had already been requisitioned by the military. In fact the Ice House at Rise was used as his explosive store. At this stage it appeared that he controlled only the county area as far as Bainton, the northern section coming under the command of Captain Atkinson, the North Riding Intelligence Officer whose HQ was at Danby Lodge, Danby. A contemporary map shows East and North Ridings as part of the same Area No.3.

In the event of an invasion, the Rise HQ was ultimately provided with its own underground observation base (OB). Unlike the standard patrol OB, just of sufficient size to accommodate seven men, Captain Hollis's OB was much larger, and in comparative terms could be described as the 'Hilton or Ritz' of OBs. Being the HQ OB its size would be dictated by the need to both accommodate additional stores for the county patrols and for any patrol members whose own OB had been either discovered or destroyed.

From the brick lined entrance shaft to the exit shaft this HQ bunker was 128ft (39m) in length. The first section consisted of a half round corrugated steel, Nissen type chamber 43ft (13m) in length and 9'.6" (2.9m) wide. This was the main accommodation area, which at date of survey (1995) still contained six timber framed double bunk beds. Ventilation was provided by saltglazed pipes at both ends. Two separate overhead manifold sets of pipes appear to have been inserted in the steel roof at a later date. The reason for this may have been the near death of a party of visiting soldiers who were apparently pulled out, almost unconscious following a weekend underground.

The next chamber, a flat roof section with brick walls provided the ablution area. This contained two separate taps (both cold!) set into the brickwall fed from concealed overhead water tanks. These tanks, set in a brick lined chamber, were refilled via camouflaged hatches at ground level. This ablution area possibly contained the chemical toilets. From this led a half round, corrugated steel, tunnel, for a distance of 28'.6" (8.7m). At 4'.7" (1.3m) in height it was possible for the average man to walk in a stooping position. At the end of this tunnel was a small square brick chamber containing ventilation pipes and a soak away sump in the floor. Branching out from this chamber were two further tunnels. The shorter one appears to have been either an abandoned working or storage area for explosives. The larger tunnel, some 27' (8.2m) in length, turns off at right angles leading to a brick lined escape hatch. Whilst both the original entrance and escape hatches have long since disappeared, the presence of two heavy specially modified cast iron gate finials suggest a cantilevered opening hatch system.

Middleton Hall, at Middleton on the Wolds, was the next location for the County HQ. This move possibly in late 41, early 1942, may have been prompted by the East Riding becoming a separate Auxiliary Area, and breaking away from North Riding. Middleton on the Wolds, by its very name was the central point of the county, and ideal for the County HQ. Another strategic reason could have been that Rise HQ was possibly too close to the coast, and thus communication with inland divisional HQs would have been more difficult to maintain in the event of an invasion.

Like Rise, an underground OB was built for Captain Hollis and his HQ within the grounds of Middleton Hall. The original OB at Rise was then handed over to the Skirlaugh Patrol. Once again the new OB was constructed to a high standard incorporating features not previously adopted

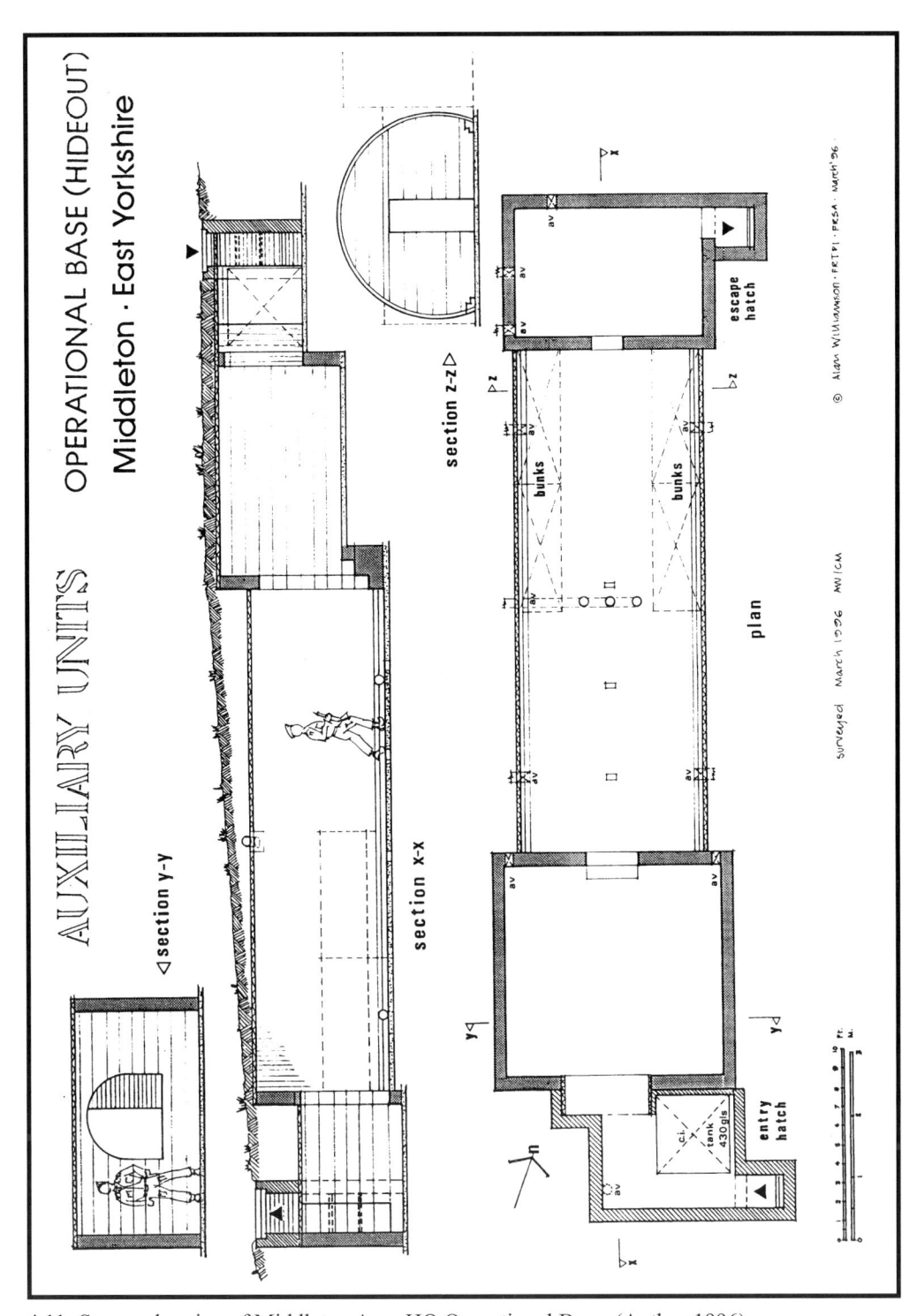

4.11 Survey drawing of Middleton Aux. HQ Operational Base. (Author 1996)

in earlier OBs. For the first time a stepped foundation system was used negating the need to dig deep on a sloping site. As a result the floor levels for each compartment descended towards the escape hatch. The complete bunker, comprising four chambers was 52ft (15.8m) in length, the entry and escape hatches being incorporated within the main chambers without the need for tunnels. The principal accommodation consisted of a half round, corrugated steel, Nissen type hut, 26'.6" (8m) long. Surviving features indicate that it was fitted out with four timber double bunk beds. Square post holes in the floor appear to point to there being a long central table, min 10'.6" (3.2m) long. At either end of the Nissen structure is a rectangular, flat roofed chamber with concrete block walls, the first chamber, which is brick lined houses the entrance hatch and a 430gal. (1628 lte) cast iron water tank. Overall it provided a higher standard of accommodation with an improved ventilation system.

In 1942, having established the East Riding organisation, Captain Hollis volunteered to join the East African Rifles in Kenya. His earlier guerrilla training obviously assisted in him being chosen to lead a secret landing party on Madagascar to check reports of a Japanese submarine servicing base. In this respect, Peter Hollis has confirmed he is the former Intelligence Officer, mentioned in David Lampe's book *The Last Ditch* p.150. After service in India and Burma, he followed his father's profession into the Church of England.

The role of East Riding Intelligence Officer was taken over by a Captain Terry Leigh-Lye. By coincidence he was also son of a vicar. Coming from Somerset and following a public school and University education, he became well known as a boxing journalist. Though an amateur boxer he also had some professional bouts. With such skills he acquitted himself quite well in unarmed combat training, as many East Riding Auxiliary Unit members can painfully testify. He remained the Intelligence Officer until the D-Day invasion of France. Between 1955 and 1968 he was a regular inter round commentator for BBC Radio boxing programmes.

By 1942 the East Riding Auxiliary Units consisted of 214 men divided into 34 patrols. For ease of administration several patrols were eventually grouped together under a Group Commander to form 9 separate groups. Whilst the number in the patrol would vary due to call up for military service etc, the total number never appeared to have exceeded 214. One isolated patrol never formed part of the Group system, instead taking its orders direct from the County IO. Later on, as regular training officers and troops were being withdrawn for D-Day purposes, the Group Commanders began to take a more active administrative role. The County organisation was then divided into two areas, north and south, with two Group Commanders promoted to Area Commanders, each responsible for half the County.

The average age of the East Riding patrol members, in 1942, was 31 years, the oldest being 54 and the youngest just 16. There were only six members over the age of 50. For clarification, the dates of birth, where known, are listed under each separate patrol.

It is interesting to note, that like Coleshill, the Middleton HQ postal address was c/o the local Post Office.

5. East Riding Patrols

5.1 Northern Area

The Northern Area consisted of 16 patrols forming four Groups (Nos. 1 – 4).

The Area Group Commander was Captain Charles V. Colley of Bridlington, whose occupation was described as a cook and confectioner. He was also Group Commander for No1 Group. His Assistant Group Commander was Lieut. Neville J. Woodward, the proprietor of the Brunswick Hotel, Bridlington.

The Group Sgt. Clerks were Sgt. Jeffrey Horsfield and Sgt. William M. Jacob, both of Bridlington. The Training W.O was C.S.M Frederick K. Richardson, also of Bridlington.

Group No.1, consisted of the following patrols:-

Bridlington North Patrol

Patrol Members (1942 list)	Civilian Occupation	Date of Birth
Sgt. Albert Berry	Motor Engineer	5.6.1893
Cpl. George H Parkin	Haulage contractor	24.6.1905
Pte. John Woodcock	Farmer	15.1.1924
Pte. George Robson	Farmer	14.12.1907
Pte. Lancelot W Colville	Farm Worker	3.3.1916

The Patrol OB was built in the side of a small chalk pit, within a small copse of trees near Marton Lodge, to the north of Martongate, Bridlington.

The OB was unusual in that it was built entirely in brick, with a flat re-inforced concrete roof, and divided into two rooms, one of which formed the entrance.

Mr John Woodcock, the one surviving patrol member available for interview, recalled it being built by both members of the Army Pioneer Corps and the Royal Engineers. To disguise its construction from the air, a camouflage net slung between the nearby trees covered the whole operation. The escape tunnel was built above ground and covered with the excavated chalk and rubble and earth. The OP was in a hollow tree trunk alongside the main road (Martongate) and linked to the OB by field telephone.

Today the OB remains substantially intact, although the escape tunnel end has either been destroyed or covered with tipped material. John Woodcock, as a 16 year old teenager, secretly watched the OB being built on his father's farm. The patrol, apparently, decided that the best way of keeping his silence was to make him a member. Therefore at 16, he became the youngest member of the East Riding Auxiliary Unit.

Bridlington South Patrol

Patrol Members (1942 list)	Civilian Occupation	Date of Birth
Sgt. Percy J Wardill	Boot Repairer	14.4.1909
Pte. Eric W Newlove	Market Gardener	10.12.1920
Pte. Harold Newlove	Market Gardener	19.4.1910
Pte. Frank Withernwick	Plumber	1.1.1915

AUXILIARY UNITS

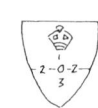

OPERATIONAL BASE
Bridlington North

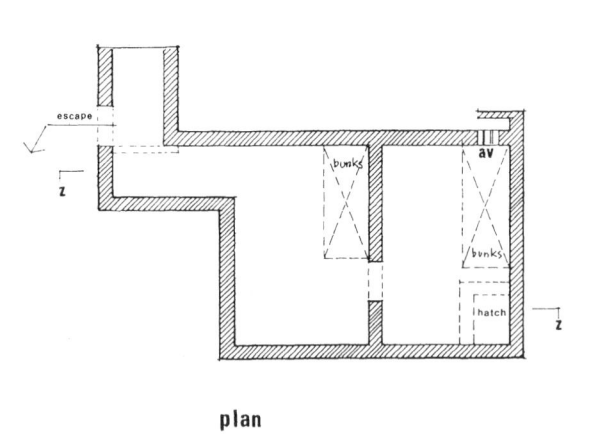

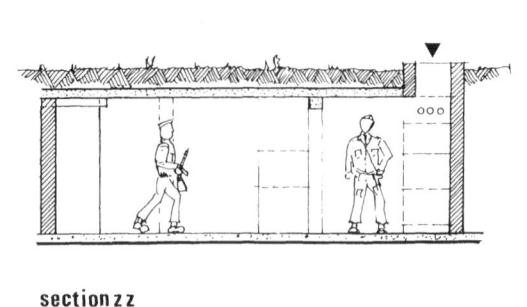

plan

section zz

surveyed April 1996 © Alan Williamson FRTPI Rtd
January 2003

5.1 Survey drawing of Bridlington North Patrol OB. (Author 2003)

5.2 Charlie Mason with John Woodcock (Bridlington North Patrol) at the entrance to his OB. (Author 1999)

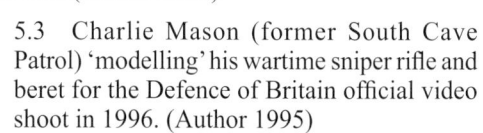

5.3 Charlie Mason (former South Cave Patrol) 'modelling' his wartime sniper rifle and beret for the Defence of Britain official video shoot in 1996. (Author 1995)

The original patrol leader was Sgt Woodward (later Lieut. Woodward, Assistant Area Group Commander). A Pte John Baron may also have been an earlier member.

No surviving member could be traced for interview. The OB, apparently a MkI version, had been built into the eastern bank of Burton Drain, to the west of Bridlington Road, Barmston. A site inspection revealed that the OB had been destroyed leaving a small depression in the bank side.

Burton Fleming Patrol

Patrol Members (1942 list)	Civilian Occupation	Date of Birth
Sgt. George E Pickering	Lorry Driver	3.10.1911
Cpl. George Boyes	Machine Fitter	21.10.1921
Pte. Wilfred Allison	Farm Worker	28.7.1920
Pte. William K Wells	Farmer	20.7.1923

Pte Tom Wells, Pte Kenneth Burrell and Pte Allen Harvey appear to have been members until 1942.

Information on the patrol and OB was given by George Boyes in an interview at Kilham in November 1997. The OB had been built beneath the old North Burton Windmill about ½ mile (800m) north west of Burton Fleming, on the Forden road. Entrance to the OB was from inside the mill tower and the escape tunnel was outside, the exit hatch under a pile of rubble.

The OB itself was divided into 2-3 sections and the OP was nearby in an old well. Exercises were held in Campwell Dale, halfway to Flixton. They had joint manoeuvres with the Flixton Patrol.

George Boyes was initially in the Home Guard for a short period, as were the other members of the patrol. He remembered that they had a Tommy guns, later replaced with Stenguns. They also had 0.38 revolvers and a commando knife.

The old mill is now demolished, and there is no site evidence of the OB or OP.

Burton Agnes Patrol

Patrol Members (1942 List)	Civilian Occupation	Date of Birth
Sgt. Charles H Wardill	Pork Butcher	14.10.1901
Cpl. Robert W Noble	Agricultural Worker	25.6.1915
Pte. Wilfred S Wright	Agricultural Worker	10.5.1906
Pte. Leonard R Wilson	Agricultural Worker	9.3.1925
Pte. Cecil A Winter	Agricultural Worker	28.12.1916
Pte. Kenneth G Cooper	Agricultural Worker	16.5.1923

Sgt. Frederick Dixon, the Burton Agnes Stationmaster, was the original patrol leader. Another early member was Pte. David Rogerson.

The OB was in Stone Pit Plantation, to the north of Burton Agnes. The original MkI OB was close to the roadside, but this later replaced with a MkII Nissen hut version on the east side of the pit. No sign remains of the MkI, but the brick end walls of the MkII are still in evidence. It would appear that the OB had been demolished with explosives.

The location of the OBs was provided by Ken Cooper, the last surviving member of the patrol on a site visit carried out in October 1994. He recalled training at Middleton Hall and Rudston Parva Quarry. Their equipment included 9mm revolvers, commando knives, 2 Tommy guns (later replaced with Sten guns, knuckle dusters and a 0.22 silenced sniper rifle.

Kilham Patrol

Patrol Members (1942 List)	Civilian Occupation	Date of Birth
Sgt. Harry Middlewood	Agricultural Worker	3.5.1915
Cpl. Leslie R Smith	Agricultural Worker	23.2.1922
Pte. Philip Wilson	Agricultural Worker	15.9.1909
Pte. Arthur H Carr	Agricultural Worker	29.10.1921
Pte. Donald Wilson	Agricultural Worker	5.8.1908
Pte. Douglas W Gray	Agricultural Worker	13.11.1918

The OB was in an old chalkpit near Keeper's House on the north west side of Kilham Lane. Arthur Carr, the one surviving patrol member, when interviewed in November 1997, confirmed that the OB was a simple square dugout (MkI) with chalk sides. Entrance was via steps but there was no escape tunnel or hatch, and ventilation consisted of an air vent in the roof.

A site inspection on 27th November 1997 showed that the OB had been destroyed, leaving a deep depression with a small section of corrugated iron. This was a good location being about halfway between the villages of Kilham and Rudston.

Flixton Patrol

Patrol Members (1942 List)	Civilian Occupation	Date of Birth
Sgt. William H Found	Farmer	8.3.1903
Cpl. Eric Barker	Gardener	9.8.1914
Pte. Jack Rudd	Farmer	6.2.1904
Pte. George Ellis	Farmer	31.10.1909
Pte. Jack Stephenson	Gardener	10.10.1920
Pte. George W Sellers	Farm Worker	29.3.1910
Pte. John O Tindall	Tractor Driver	26.7.1918

The original patrol leader was Sergeant Charles Henry Moxlow, a Flixton grocer, who unfortunately died following a car accident at Middleton on the Wolds, during a training exercise, on the 27th June 1942. He was 33 years old at the time, and was about to be promoted to Lieutenant. This would in effect have made him a Group Leader, possibly in charge of the Flixton, Burton Fleming and Wold Newton Patrols. These patrols worked together, but were integrated into an oversized group (No1) consisting of a staggering eight separate patrols.

One interesting carbon copy of a letter from Sgt Moxlow to a Cpl Phillips has survived. From another source Cpl Phillips has been identified as a Musketry Instructor on Captain Hollis's HQ staff. The letter set out below is interesting as it shows the type of transport being used by the Flixton patrol. The OB was located in a small copse at Flixton Brow. It consisted of a standard Nissen hut type structure (MkII), with an escape tunnel running down the hillside. When inspected in April 1998 the bunker had been partially destroyed with the remaining section of the corrugated steel roof in a dangerous condition. It is understood that it has now completely collapsed. The site was in an excellent location, being in an elevated position overlooking the main road (A1039) leading from the coast. It is also close to RAF Staxton Wold radar station.

> The Stores
> Flixton
>
> 13/6/42
>
> Cpl Phillips
>
> Dear Frank
>
> Please find enclosed receipt for Peter's revolver for petrol coupons allocated. The registration numbers for Ellis's & Barker's requiring petrol coupons are Ellis VH 5241 Hillman 10HP / and Barker VH 4060 Jowett 8HP.
> Would you please confirm for me from Capt. Leigh-Lye when our weekly training is to take place. I am of the opinion that Capt. Leigh-Lye changed the day from Thursday to Wednesday, as Wednesday is more convenient to Burton Fleming people but Lieut Laurens thinks it is still Thursday.

> SUBJECT:- Petrol Coupons, December 41.
> To:- Mr. Moxlow, Flixton   ER 19
>
> Herewith petrol coupons for this month. Please sign the attached receipt and return to me immediately.
>
> The Regd. No. of the car should be inserted on the coupon before it is presented, and, together with the H.P., on the petrol return and ~~M. O. 1771~~. The petrol return must be completed in every detail and returned to me by the 28th day of the month. Future petrol supplies must be contingent on the careful observation of these instructions.
>
> c/o GPO,
> Middleton-on-the-Wolds,
> Driffield, Yorks.   P. Hollis Captain,
> 5/12/41.   I. O. East Riding Area.

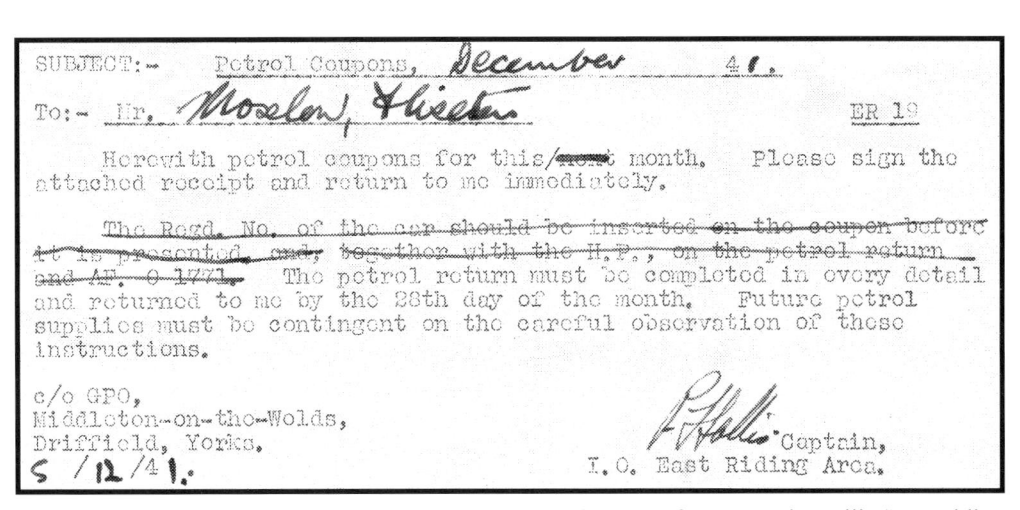

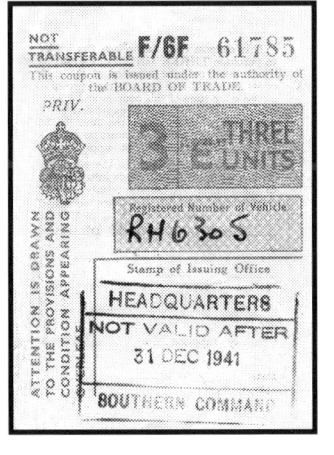

5.4 Instructions dated 5.12.41 from Captain Hollis (East Riding Intelligence Officer to Mr Moxlow (Flixton Patrol Leader) re petrol coupons. Note Captain Hollis's address is c/o GPO not Middleton Hall. (Edward Moxlow coll.)

5.5 Actual petrol coupon retained by Mr Moxlow, possibly one of those referred to in Captains Hollis' note of 5.12.41. (Edward Moxlow coll.)

FLIXTON HOME GUARD OFFICER'S DEATH

Inquest Opened On Victim of Car Accident

An inquest was opened at Driffield on Tuesday on Charles Henry Moxlow (33), grocer, of The Stores, Flixton, an acting-lieutenant in the Home Guard, who was fatally injured when thrown from a motor-car during Home Guard exercises near Middleton-on-the-Wolds, on Saturday night.

Moxlow, a married man, with one child, was a native of Pudsey, and joined the Home Guard soon after war broke out. He had been informed of promotion from sergeant to lieutenant a few days before the tragedy.

The Deputy Coroner (Mr. H. W. Rennison) took only evidence of identification before adjourning the inquiry to Wednesday, July 8th, at 2.30 p.m.

John Thomas Found, farmer, of Church Farm, Folkton, stated that Moxlow was his son-in-law, and assisted him on the farm, while Mrs. Moxlow assisted at the grocer's shop. He last saw Moxlow about 10 a.m. on the day of the accident, before deceased left to go on a Home Guard exercise. He had since seen Moxlow's body at the Alfred Bean Hospital, Driffield.

It is understood that Moxlow was in a car driven by an officer, and accompanied by a sergeant and lance-corporal in the Regular Army, and Moxlow was thrown from the vehicle on to the road while the driver was turning a sharp bend on the outskirts of Middleton village. Sergt. Verity, one of the occupants, received slight injury. Moxlow was unconscious when picked up, and he died about a quarter of an hour afterwards.

THE FUNERAL

The funeral took place at Folkton on Wednesday afternoon. The Rev. W. H. Wall officiated, and a large number attended.

The chief mourners were: Mrs. C. Moxlow (wife); Mrs. Moxlow, Pudsey (mother); Mr. J. Moxlow (brother); Mr. and Mrs. J. F. Found (father-in-law and mother-in-law); Mr. W. H. Found (brother-in-law); Mr. F. Found (brother-in-law); Miss E. Found (sister-in-law).

Among those present were Captain Leigh-Lye, Lieut. Laurens, and the 1st Platoon Home Guard, members of a Searchlight Unit, A.R.P. members, and Special Constables.

Among those who sent floral tokens were Capt. Leigh-Lye and Lieut. Lawrens; Commanding Officer and Men of the "A" Unit; "His Pals in the H.G." "No. 1 Platoon H.G." and Workmen from Church Farm.

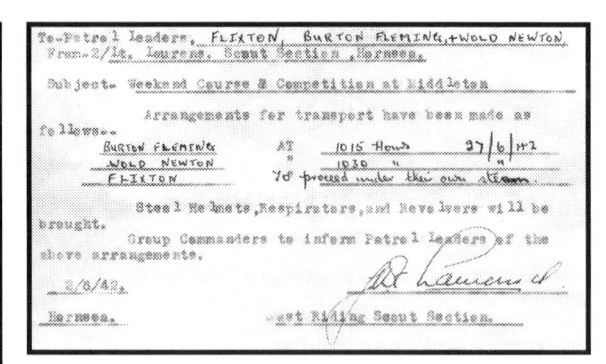

5.6 Orders from Lt Lauren, East Riding Scout Section for Flixton, Burton Fleming & Wold Newton Patrols to attend weekend training on 27.6.42. This copy was sent to Sgt Charles Moxlow (Flixton Patrol).
(Edward Moxlow coll.)

5.7 Newspaper report of the death of Sgt Charles Moxlow on 27.6.42. (Edward Moxlow coll.)

5.8 Sgt Charles Moxlow with 'friends', helping on his father-in-law's farm, in about 1939/40.
(Edward Moxlow coll.)

Wold Newton Patrol

Patrol Members (1942 List)	Civilian Occupation	Date of Birth
Sgt. Louis Chapman	Farmer	15.8.1892
Cpl. Henry Streets	Farm Worker	17.7.1914
Pte. Arthur W Sellers	Farm Worker	31.8.1914
Pte. Fred Sellers	Farm Worker	28.9.1926
Pte. John T Elgey (?)	Farmer	19.5.1914

Location of the OB was understood to be in a quarry on the west side of the Fordon road, some 200 yards (180m) to the north of the village. Today the quarry has been filled, and there is now no sign of the OB. The Pte. John Elgey referred to was a member of Bainton Patrol, as was his brother James. No surviving members have been found for interview.

However, the late Henry Street's daughter has sent a copy of his Home Guard Certificate which lists his service from 6th June 1942 until 31st December 1944. These dates will refer to his time with the Auxiliary Units.

The Wold Newton patrol appeared to be in trouble on one occasion by being absent from a Group lecture. The following letter sent to the patrol leader by Sgt Moxlow sets out the circumstances:

The Stores
Flixton

13/6/42

Sergt. Green, Wold Newton Patrol

Dear George

    Mr Laurens was out here on Wednesday evening to give a lecture to the Group at Danesbury Manor as arranged by Capt. Leigh-Lye on his last visit. As your patrol were not present I am ordered by Lieut. Laurens to write for the reason of your absence. Please write by return for me to send to Lieut Laurens for his next visit.

    Yours sincerely

    Charles Moxlow (Sergt)

What the reply to this letter was we shall probably never know. What is more intriguing is who was Sgt Green? His name has never appeared on any list nor mentioned by any surviving members of the Group. However, it shows that Sgt Moxlow was probably acting in the capacity of a Group Leader.

5.09 Charlie Mason points to the escape tunnel entrance in the partially destroyed Flixton OB. The roof has now completely collapsed. (Author 1998)

5.10 Sgt William Found (Flixton Patrol), brother in law of Sgt Charles Moxlow. (Brian Found coll.)

Harpham Patrol

Patrol Members (1942 List)	Civilian Occupation	Date of Birth
Sgt. Robert Pearson	-	-
Cpt. Frank Garton	Farmer	21.12.1916
Pte. Thomas Webster	Farmer	15.6.1915
Pte. Ronald Sellers	-	-
Pte. Raymond Sellers	-	-

No surviving members have been found for interview. The OB may have been somewhere in the Gransmoor Gravel Pits.

Group No.2, consisting of the Norton, Settrington and Scampston patrols was commanded by Lieut. Henry Towse, the Scampston gamekeeper. He was born in October 1904.

Norton Patrol

Patrol Members (1942 List)	Civilian Occupation	Date of Birth
Sgt. John S Boggitt	Farm Foreman	15.11.1913
Cpl. William E Williams	Lorry Driver	28.12.1912
Pte. John Foord	General Labourer	16.12.1906

Earlier members had been Pte. Arthur B. Barker, Pte. James B. Barker and Pte. Kenneth Weatherill.

No surviving members were found for interview but Alan Gibson of Norton recalled his schoolboy days during the war and making an unusual discovery as follows: -

Walking at the side of a wood I found what appeared to be a small length of telephone cable which disappeared into the ground. After investigation we found that this led to well concealed hatch cover in the old quarry side the roof the chamber had been created by what I believe to have been metal sheets which appeared to have been covered with wet cement and loose stone allowed to fall down on it creating a natural effect, which had grown over with moss and elderberry – there was also a second hatch at the base concealed under a bush. The whole chamber being approximately 16'x8' – the only contents as far as I can now remember were some wooden bunks, so presume by then it had been abandoned.

This appears to be a good description of an early MkI type OB situated in the side of an old quarry, near Gallows Hill to the south west of Beverley Road, Norton.

A more recent investigation of the site accompanied by Alan Gibson, failed to discover the OB, which presumably now lies destroyed beneath a partially tipped quarry. Likewise there was no sign of the telephone cable which apparently ran to an observation post (OP) near the main road.

Settrington Patrol

Patrol Members (1942 List)	Civilian Occupation	Date of Birth
Sgt. William S Eggleton	Gamekeeper	16.6.1900
Cpl. Harold Hugill	Market Gardener	4.2.1904
Pte. Roland G Walden	Farm Bailiff	3.9.1912
Pte. Charles Hodgson	Farm Labourer	13.1.1908
Pte. John J Scott	Gamekeeper	14.1.1902
Pte. Samuel R Wardell	Farmer	17.3.1911
Pte. James W Sleightholme	Shepherd	11.11.1904

A Pte. Kenneth P. Pickersgill appears to have been an earlier member of the patrol.

No surviving members have been found for interview. However, Mr. Appleyard the former Settrington Estate gamekeeper, has confirmed that the patrol's training area was in Nine Springs Dale, between Settrington and Duggleby. He also recalls finding sheets of corrugated iron some 100 yards away from the training area. This seems to suggest that there had been a Mk.II OB at this location.

5.11 Group No.3 in November 1944.
Back Row: Edgar Smallwood, Sid Hodgson, Harold Grice, Charlie Cook, Dennis Cook, (unknown).
　　　Middle Row: Doug Webster, Norman Grice, George Robson, Billie Snaith, Harold Walker, Charlie Mears.
　　　Front Row: Cpl Robert Dent, Cpl Johnson, Sgt (unknown), Lt Bob Sisterton, Sgt Milner, Sgt Harry Milson.
(Author's coll.)

Scampston Patrol

Patrol Members (1942 List)	Civilian Occupation	Date of Birth
Sgt. Joseph Allanby	Lorry Driver	15.6.1906
Cpl. Herbert Batty	Timber Man	8.12.1903
Pte. Alec Burrows	Vermin Killer	1.11.1907
Pte. Frank Burrows	Joiner	11.1.1906
Pte. Sidney Temple	Bacon Curer	15.12.1907

No surviving members have been found for interview. However with the kind permission of Sir Charles Legard, and accompanied by the present gamekeeper, Raymond Ireland, a preliminary search was made for a possible OB location. Nothing was found, but a former member of the local Home Guard recalled that the Patrol had used the Ice House, at Scampston Hall for storage of explosives etc.

Group No.3, consisting of the Leavening, Westow and Wharram patrols, was commanded by Lieut. Robert Sisterton. Described as a vermin controller, he was born in November 1909, and lived at Settrington. The Group Sgt. Clerk was Sgt. George Robson, a Porter Signalman, also from Settrington. He was born in June 1912.

Leavening Patrol

Patrol Members (1942 List)	Civilian Occupation	Date of Birth
Sgt. Percy Milner	Farmer	13.10.1898
Cpt. Robert Dent	Farmer	22.2.1914
Pte. George Robson	Farmer	4.4.1904
Pte. Norman Grice	Farm Labourer	13.4.1918
Pte. Douglas Webster	Farmer	11.12.1917
Pte. Edgar Smallwood	Farm Worker	11.11.1923
Pte. Harold Grice	Farm Labourer	7.4.1916

In an interview with former patrol member, Norman Grice, his list of members includes a Pte. Douglas Brown. No records have been found recording this name.

The original MkI OB was in Rabbit Hill a small woodland overlooking Leavening village and just below Leavening Brow. This was simple square dugout approx. 8'x8' (2.4 x 2.4m) with a roof of corrugated steel sheets containing a central vent pipe. Entrance was via a tunnel 3-4 yds (2.7-3.6m) long. There was no separate escape hatch. It was built by the Royal Engineers. The roof having collapsed it was replaced by a MkII version, some 545yds (500m) to the south in an area known as Coombs.

This MkII was the standard Nissen type with a vertical entrance hatch and an escape tunnel approx. 24yds (22m) running into a small stone pit. The entrance hatch contains steel pipe ladder rungs and a brick baffle wall. The escape tunnel made out of 3ft (0.9m) concrete culvert pipes had a bend in the middle. There was a central vent to the main chamber. Norman Grice couldn't recall any other vent pipes. It had been furnished with a table and bunks.

From an external inspection the OB appears to be in good condition, apart from the original hatches being missing. An infestation of rats prevented an internal survey.

The OP had consisted of a 2 man dugout linked by telephone, to the OB approximately 30yds (27m) to the south west, on the brow of the hill. A site inspection failed to reveal any remaining evidence.

The patrol had been issued with the standard equipment i.e. a Tommy gun, Stenguns, 0.38 Smith and Wesson revolvers, a 0.22 sniper rifle and a Canadian Ross 0.300 rifle. They also had the Fairbairn commando dagger and a cosh. Rifle training was carried out at the Guisborough Rifle Range.

Norman Grice says that they never spent a single night in the OB, but they drank all the rum! At the Stand Down, they fired off all the surplus ammunition.

5.12 Norman Grice (Leavening Patrol) at the entrance to his OB, marked by the two concrete blocks. (Author 1998)

5.13 Charlie Mason and Dennis Cook inspecting the remains of the Westow Patrol OB. (Author 1998)

Westow Patrol

Patrol Members (1942 List)	Civilian Occupation	Date of Birth
Sgt. Fred Hodgson	Labourer	3.1.1908
Pte. Sidney Hodgson	Farm Labourer	30.7.1906
Pte. Charles E Cook	Joiner	16.9.1897
Pte. Dennis W Cook	Joiner	5.5.1927

The first sergeant had been Wilfred E Parker, a Westow farmer, and the original corporal was Herbert Spenceley. At some point, Herbert Spenceley, a local tractor driver, born in August 1915, was also listed as a sergeant.

Dennis Cook, a surviving member, recalled Pte. Edgar Smallwood, a farmworker from East Acklam, as being a member of the Westow patrol. His name certainly appears in an earlier list of Auxiliary Unit members. Another earlier list, transferring members from the Home Guard, suggests that Pte. Ernest Lee, Pte. Leslie Wray, and Pte. Bernard Wardle had been original members of the Westow Patrol.

Dennis Cook, the son of Charlie Cook, another patrol member, recalls training at Wetherby. He later joined the RAF and saw service overseas.

The OB was the standard Nissen hut (MkII) variety and was located in Howsham Wood, to the west of Westow. About 219yds (220m) to the south-east was a one man OP appropriately close to Spy Hill.

Whilst the corrugated steel roof of the OB no longer remains, the 9" (228mm) end brick walls still stand. There is still evidence of an escape tunnel, measuring 11'.6' (3.5m) long. This may have been brick lined, at least on one side. The tunnel roof had been covered with flat corrugated steel sheets.

Wharram Patrol

Patrol Members (1942 List)	Civilian Occupation	Date of Birth
Sgt. Harry T Milson	Tractor Driver	29.10.1913
Cpl. Thomas Johnson	Vermin Destroyer	27.11.1908
Pte. Albert Burton	Quarry Foreman	5.2.1898
Pte. Harold Walker	Farmer	26.3.1905
Pte. George W Snaith	Motor Fitter	5.1.1926
Pte. Charles H Mears	Tractor Driver	6.4.1918

Harry Milson confirmed that their OB had been destroyed, in fact an earlier press report stated that all that remained was a small depression in the ground. The OB was situated on the east facing slope of a steep valley, to the west of Wharram le Street. In the bottom of the valley was the former Driffield to Malton railway line. To the south the railway passed through the Burdale Tunnel which was about one mile (1½km) in length. This tunnel, with the winding road on Grimston Hill, would have been ideal sabotage targets for the patrol.

The OB appeared to be a MkI type consisting of a 8ft (2.4m) square dugout lined with corrugated iron sheets and tree trunks. The concealed entrance was via a small tunnel, 9-12 ft (2.7-3.6m) long.

The tunnel entrance hatch was camouflaged with vegetation. Internal ventilation was achieved by a central pipe in the roof. There was no escape tunnel.

Harry Milson confirmed that it was built by a Royal Engineer Unit. Their training was done at Coleshill Hall, Middleton Hall and Guisborough, with infiltration exercises carried out on nearby aerodromes and Settrington Hall.

Initially in the Wharram Home Guard, Harry and his pal Bob Sisterton were both recruited by a Captain Atkinson, the original IO for the northern part of the East Riding, which in the early days was linked with North Riding.

Harry Milson had kept his wartime notebook in which he had jotted down various aspects of the patrol's activities.

One such item appears to be an inventory of the patrol (or Group) stock of equipment.

Aux Units	-	3 old T	(Boxes of explosives etc)
Ammo .300	-	798 rnds	(Ammunition)
Revolver (.38)	-	296	(")
.22 Rifle	-	550	(")
Sten Gun	-	1215	(")
Grenades	-	53	(36m Mills bomb)
Camouflage cream	-	17 tubes	
'L' Delays	-	15	(Time pencils)
Release switches	-	5	
Primers Mark II	-	10	
Smoke screens	-	4	(No 77 Smoke Grenade)
Paraffin incende	-	24	(76 grenade – AW bottle)
Pull switches	-	-	
Thunder Flashes	-	36	
Plastic sticks	-	19	(Plastic explosive)
Explosives – boxes	-	6	
—?— Aux Units	-	6	

The note book, in addition to recording all the serial numbers of each patrol members' revolver and Sten gun, contained details of some training programmes.

The one for May (year unknown) is set out below:

7th May	OB Wharram	Group explosives 10.00am
14th May	Leavening	Daylight reconnaissance 10.00am
12th May	Inspection arms 8pm	
21st May	Leavening – shooting rifle – sten 1.30pm	
24th May	Settrington – Cpl Robinson 8pm	
28th May	Course – Middleton 10.00am	
29th May	Leavening 8pm	

Group No.4, consisting of Bainton and Lockington Patrols, was commanded by Lieut. Frank Byass, a Bainton Farmer. He was born in June 1914, and was the original leader of the Bainton Patrol.

Bainton Patrol

Patrol Members (1942 List)	Civilian Occupation	Date of Birth
Sgt. David F Byass	Farmer	21.10.1916
Cpt. Harold W Barrat	Agricultural Engineer	23.3.1907
Pte. Tom F Byass	Farmer	25.6.1912
Pte. John T Elgey	Farmer	19.5.1914
Pte. Angus J Elgey	Farmer	19.9.1921
Pte. Tom H Stocks	Farmer	21.10.1906
Pte. Wilfred Simpson	Corn Merchant	

The first OB was a dugout in the side of a small disused pit adjoining Manor Farm, Bainton. Whilst a strategic position in the sense of controlling activities at the important junction of the B1248 (Beverley to Malton road) with the B1246 (Driffield to Pocklington road), its very proximity to this junction would have prevented free movement and increased the possibility of detection. It is the type of junction which would have been quickly secured by an invasion force, and thereafter, well guarded.

A replacement OB (MkII) was therefore built underground in High Wood, some 440yds (400m) to the north of Manor Farm. This consisted of a standard half round corrugated steel Nissen type bunker, with brick end walls. At the eastern end was an escape tunnel with a cast iron fresh water tank overhead. A 1" cast iron pipe fed water into the bunker.

At the other end a field telephone wire, concealed in a 3" cast iron pipe led from the bunker to an observation post (OP). The entrance hatch was hidden under a cantilevered hollowed out tree trunk. Ventilation was provided by a series of 6" (15m) SGW pipes, with the stale air being extracted via a hollow tree trunk. There was the usual OB equipment of double bunk beds and paraffin stove etc.

The one man observation post (OP) was also sited in High Wood, some 50yds (46m) back from the main road (B1248). In close proximity to the MkII OB was a second underground structure made out of Stanton concrete arch sections, and apparently entered by a 20ft (6m) tunnel. This may have been a separate store for explosives and ammunition.

The location of the MkII OB was close to a public footpath which afforded access without undue disturbance of the surrounding vegetation. High Wood itself gave good cover for crossing the high ground leading to the Driffield Airfield, about 1½ miles (2.4km) to the east. Both Driffield and Leconfield RAF stations were covertly entered as part of the patrol's training for attacking aircraft and other installations.

The patrol's initial equipment included the American Browning Automatic rifle (BAR) as well as 9mm revolvers, a 0.22 sniper rifle and the Thompson machine gun (Tommy Gun). The latter gun was later replaced by the Sten gun. In addition to the Fairbairn commando knife they had 'knuckle dusters' obviously of local origin, as not being known as standard issue equipment.

5.14 John Elgey (Bainton Patrol) with the remains of his OB. (Author 1995)

5.16 Charlie Mason at the destroyed Bainton Patrol OB. (Author 2000)

5.15 George Harrison (Lockington Patrol) on the site of the Patrol's OP. (Author 1995)

Today the High Wood OB is still quite visible, with most of the corrugated roof caved in due the felling of a nearby mature tree. A section of the field telephone line is still visible in the CI pipe leading from the entrance. The water tank still remains but not quite in its original position.

The only remains of the explosive store (?) and tunnel is an 'L' shaped depression in the ground and scattered broken sections of the Stanton concrete panels. The OP being a simple small foxhole has long since disappeared.

Much helpful information was given by the three surviving members of the original patrol, namely John Elgey, Frank and David Byass.

Frank Byass is the only surviving Group Leader in the East Riding.

Lockington Patrol

Patrol Members (1942 List)	Civilian Occupation	Date of Birth
Sgt. William Walmsley	Woodman	30.4.1907
Cpl. Thomas Hill	Farm Worker	14.2.1914
Pte. Leonard Hill	Farm Worker	22.8.1923
Pte. George Brayshaw	Farm Worker	27.8.1920
Pte. George A Harrison	Farm Worker	12.2.1921
Pte. Arthur Clubley	Farm Foreman	16.11.1920
Pte. George A Nicholson	-	-

George Harrison, one of the two surviving members, recalled that two other early members of the patrol had been George Watson (Lockington joiner), who was called up for active service, and Clarence Hudson. He also remembered that a Corporal Phillips was the small arms instructor at the Middleton HQ.

They were issued with the standard equipment i.e. one Tommy Gun, revolvers, rifles, Sten guns and commando knives. The only non-standard item was the ligature, which one or two other patrols adopted.

Their OB was a MkI version built into the side of a small chalk quarry, about one mile (1.6km) to the west of Beswick village. It appeared to be a simple dugout, measuring 17ft x 10ft (5.2m x 3m). The walls and roof were made of flat corrugated sheets buttressed with timber posts.

The main access was direct into the OB via a wooden ladder, with a key to the hatch hidden under some turf. The internal height was thought to be 6'6" (1.98m) and the floor level 10ft (3m) below ground level.

Ken Suggitt, the former quarry owner, who destroyed the bunker himself, confirmed that the roof was corrugated iron sheeting carried on timber poles, and covered with soil/turf. George Harrison suggested that the escape tunnel had been about 30ft (9m) in length and made of similar material to the bunker. They had four bunks, a stove and an inside water tank.

The one man observation post (OP) was on the opposite of the quarry and linked by field telephone.

The OB was ideally located for sabotage operations either on the Hutton Cranswick airfield, to the north or the main Hull to Scarborough railway line to the east.

Today, all that remains of the OB is a larger depression in the ground, with some vertical timber posts still in place. Some evidence of the tunnel still shows, but measures only about 21ft (6.4m). The OP is still marked by a small depression in the quarry side.

5.18 Interior of Bewholme Patrol OB showing original MkI OB roof collapsed in the background. (Author 1995)

5.19 Charlie Mason in the remains of Bewholme Patrol OP. (Author 1995)

5.17 Stuart Elliot (local farmer) at the present day access into the Bewholme OB. (Author 1995)

5.2 Southern Area

The Southern Area consisted of 17 patrols forming five groups (Nos 5 – 9)

The Area Group Commander was Captain Walter Kitching (born 7/8/1897) who was Steward to the Grimston Estate. He was also Group Commander of No. 5 group. His assistant Area Group Commander was Captain Carrington, a leather sales manager with the local Beverley tannery. He was born in December 1899 and was also Group Commander of No. 7 group.

Group No.5, consisted of the Bewholme, Catwick, Skirlaugh, Aldbrough and Hornsea patrols. The Group Sgt. Clerk was Sgt. Robert G Hugill, an engineer from Seaton.

Bewholme Patrol

Patrol Members (1944 list)	Civilian Occupation	Date of Birth
Sgt. Walter E Varley	Farmer	14.10.1917
Cpl. Edward Rafton	Farm Worker	17.11.1916
Pte. Gordon A Varley	Farmer	01.11.1915
Pte. Claude Varley	Farmer	08.02.1924
Pte. Reginald A Hara	-	-
Pte. Reginald C Hara	Farmer	17.11.1903
Pte. Robert H Jackson	-	-

Other original members had been Sgt. F D Blanchard, a tractor driver born 6/6/1916, and Pte. Leslie Ulliott. Claude Varley and Frank Blanchard, the two surviving members provided much helpful infromation.

The OB or hideout was located to the south of Nook Lane about 1km south east of Bewholme village, and was built into the bank of a deep ditch at the junction with a field boundary hedge.

Originally it consisted of a simple MkI dugout, 10ft (3m) square with entrance direct from the ditch side. Later a MkII Nissen type bunker was built alongside; retaining the earlier dugout as the entrance, with an additional escape tunnel also built into the ditch side. The end walls were built in brick. With internal measurements of 19' x 10' (5.9m x 3m) it had originally contained 3 double bunk beds. Standard ventilation sgw pipes were built into either end with an additional pipe pushed through the corrugated steel side leading into the ditch. Apart from acting as a ventilation pipe this would prove to be an effective wastewater disposal point.

An observation post (OP) was concealed in a ditch some 200m to the east of the OB. Entrance was via a 2ft (0.6m) diameter concrete culvert pipe under a field bridge. The bridge crossing had been extended to form a small 1-man chamber with the drain water being cleverly diverted by a smaller pipe to keep the OP dry. On higher ground than the OB it gave a good view of the possible invasion coastline 3 miles to the east. The OP was linked to the OB by a hidden field telephone cable.

A separate store for explosives/ammunition was sited 50 yds (45m) to the south of the OB in an adjoining grass field.

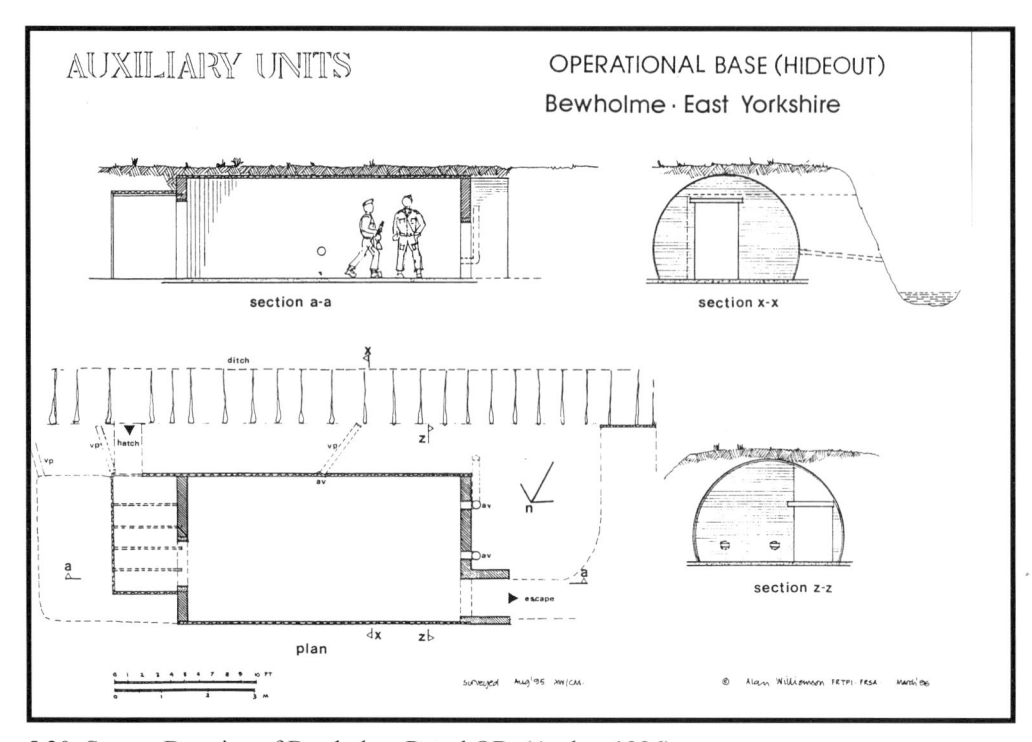

5.20 Survey Drawing of Bewholme Patrol OB. (Author 1996)

The original Patrol leader chose the OB location due to its proximity to the former Catfoss Airfield, an obvious target for any invasion force. A series of deep ditches gave direct access to the airfield from the OB. This concealed approach was apparently used on many occasions during training operations without discovery. In addition a nearby road culvert, under the main road (Nook Lane) leading from the coast to Catfoss Airfield contained demolition charges which could be activated by the patrol members.

The patrol's equipment appeared to have been standard issue, each man having a .38 revolver and fighting knife. Originally issued with one Thompson Machine Gun, the patrol members eventually had their own sten guns. The patrol also had a .22-calibre sniper rifle fitted with a silencer. They were issued with rubber agricultural type boots in addition to the standard leather army boots.

In more recent times, removal of the adjoining field hedge allowed access for heavy farm vehicles thus causing the collapse of the OB entrance hatch and exit tunnel. The main chamber, consisting of heavy gauge curved steel sections, survived but became somewhat misshapen due to the heavy overhead pressures. A small hole in an end brick wall, at the junction with the roof, is now the only access. However, this is more suitable for foxes then human beings. Timber remains of the wooden entrance are visible in the ditch side, as also are some sections of vertical, corrugated steel revetting to the escape tunnel exit.

The OP culvert entrance still remains, but the original, flimsy, concealed chamber roof has collapsed. There is no sign of the separate explosive store, the field now being in arable cultivation.

Catwick Patrol

Patrol Members (1944 List)	Civilian Occupation	Date of Birth
Sgt Gordon T Speed	Farmer	30.11.1919
Cpl John E Richardson	Farmer	08.12.1917
Pte George A Hill	Farmer	04.01.1908
Pte Kenneth Newton	Farm Worker	12.08.1913
Pte John C Hodgson	Farmer	01.07.1914
Pte Harry Thompson	Farming	16.02.1922

It is understood that the OB was constructed in the Brandesburton sand and gravel pits, but has since been destroyed.
No surviving member has been located for interview.
A Pte. Robert Hugill may have been an earlier member of the patrol.

Skirlaugh Patrol

Patrol Members (1944 List)	Civilian Occupation	Date of Birth
Sgt William U Myers	Land Draining	16.04.1895
Cpl Joe Robson	Threshing foreman	07.12.1916
Pte John Clubley	-	-
Pte Arthur Reap	-	-

5.21 Charlie Mason in the destroyed Skirlaugh Patrol OB. (Author 1996)

5.22 Charlie Mason inspecting the remains of the Aldborough Patrol's MkI OB. (Author 1994)

An original member of the patrol was Cpl. Arthur Clubley, who had moved from Skirlaugh to Hutton Cranswick. Other members were Pte. Eric Curtis, Pte. Harry Guy and Pte. Harry Martin.

Arthur Clubley, the one surviving member available for interview, provided much helpful information on the patrol, and suggests that G Decent and K Bryant had been in the patrol. Unfortunately no record can be found of these two names.

Their original OB had been in a field adjoining Benningholme Hall. It had consisted of a 12ft (3.6m) square dugout covered with 2 layers of wire netting carried on wood poles, the entrance door was made of lathed wood. This was a MkI type.

A new OB (MkII) was then built into the bank of the Swine, Benningholme and Arnold Ings drain some 650ft (595m) to the southwest. The OB was near a small copse of trees known as Minster Hill. The escape tunnel ran direct into the drain. The OB has been destroyed leaving a large depression in the ground.

A reserve of explosives and ammunition was kept in a garden shed at Springfield House, Skirlaugh.

Arthur Clubley, being one of the tallest members in the East Riding, was selected by Captain Terry Leigh-Lye, the County IO, to be his bodyguard or minder. He had retained copies of the military Ordinance Survey maps which he carried for Captain Leigh-Lye.

The patrol's equipment was fairly standard in that they had the Canadian Ross .30 rifle, revolvers, commando knives, Sten guns and the 22-sniper rifle. The only variation in equipment was that they had rubber coshes.

After the County HQ moved to Middleton-on-the-Wolds, the Skirlaugh Patrol took over the IO's bunker at Rise.

Once again Arthur Clubley made reference to the Burton Constable gamekeeper, who whilst not a patrol member, obviously assisted in their training.

Aldbrough Patrol

Patrol Members (1944 List)	Civilian Occupation	Date of Birth
Sgt Richard M Crawforth	Farmer	08.05.1922
Cpl Walter H Fisher	Farm Worker	14.04.1912
Pte Eric Beadle	Farm Worker	07.11.1924
Pte George Crawforth	Farmer	29.01.1914
Pte Frank Wood	Min of Agr. Official	12.02.1891
Pte Kenneth S Burrell	Tractor Driver	08.06.1925
Pte Frank D Blanchard	Tractor Driver	06.06.1916

It would appear that Pte. Frank Blanchard was at some time a member of Bewholme patrol. Corporal Kenneth Foot, Schoolhouse, Grimston is also listed as an earlier member.

The only surviving member for interview was George Crawforth, a retired farmer, then living at East Newton. During his service with the patrol he was farming at Cold Harbour Farm, Fitling. His brother Richard was the patrol leader and farmed at Bail House, Garton.

The OB was located in Bail Wood, about ½ miles (0.8 km) to the north east of Cold Harbour Farm. Bail Wood was almost 1 1/3 miles (2 km) to the south of Aldbrough, and a similar distance from the coast. On the western most edge of Bail Wood there are the remains of a destroyed bunker built into the top of the Bail Drain bank. Loose brickwork and fragments of corrugated steel still remain in a depression measuring roughly 20' x 10' (6m x 3m). There is also evidence of a curved escape tunnel measuring about 23' (7m) in length.

This has all the appearance of a MkI OB but George Crawforth could not recall its existence. However, towards the centre of Bail Wood is the site of a further OB which apparently still exists underground. This unfortunately has been sealed with a concrete capping for safety reasons.

George Crawforth confirmed that this was a standard Nissen type structure, with a vertical entrance shaft and a diagonal escape tunnel. Jim Rockett, who had entered the bunker prior to capping has described it as a concrete structure, about 12ft (3.6m) wide and 20ft (6.0m) in length, and 7ft (2.1m) high. It also had an escape tunnel, 3ft (0.9) square and 25yds (22.8m) in length. He recalled entering by a metal ladder, and there being a baffle wall at the bottom. Bunk beds lined both walls.

From its description, it is very much like a MkIII OB, in that the reference to concrete suggests that the end walls etc were constructed in concrete blocks. The use of concrete blocks only appears in later MkIII OBs.

Their equipment appeared to be fairly standard i.e. revolvers, Sten guns, sticky bombs and hand grenades. Although George Crawforth did mention a 2ft (0.6m) rubber cosh which he described as a most 'lethal' weapon.

Training was carried out at Middleton and Rise Park. During the War, George was only aware of other patrols at Sunk Island and Catwick.

Hornsea Patrol

Patrol Members (1944 List)	Civilian Occupation	Date of Birth
Sgt Stanley G French	Dental Surgeon	28.02.1898
Cpl Arthur S Pratt	Machine Organiser	21.10.1888
Pte George R Dowson	Clerk	07.08.1889
Pte Robert F Bell	Pig Farmer	17.04.1905
Pte Barrie Shaw-Maclean	Civil Engineer	23.12.1903
Pte Frank Hartley	Clerk	15.07.1890
Pte Stanley F Cookson	Accountant	06.05.1996

An earlier member of the patrol was Allanson Hick, an architect, and a founder member of the Royal Society of Marine Artists. This patrol appeared to have a high number of professional members with only one connected with farming.

The OB was situated in a small copse about ½ mile (0.8 km) south of Hornsea Mere near Goxhill.

When first seen, the bunker, which had been destroyed, was thought to be a Home Guard or regular military structure due to its robust construction with a bomb proof roof carried on heavy girders.

However, by chance, the original construction drawing has survived. It had been retained by Captain Kirk Chapel, the Royal Engineers officer responsible for its construction, and after his death was kept by his widow Joy, the sister of Captain Peter Hollis, the original East Riding Intelligence Officer.

Surprisingly the drawing was not a War Department plan, but was prepared by local Hull architect, Allanson Hick FRIBA, an original member of the patrol. This must be the first occasion that a member had designed his own OB. The actual drawing is entitled a "Home Guard S.P.", which disguises its true nature.

The walls are unusually thick, consisting of two skins, one single brick and one double brick, with a bitumen felt vertical damp proof membrane. The roof was 6" (152mm) reinforced concrete carried on inset railway steel girders. The plan was 'L' shaped with both entrance and escape tunnels, described on the drawing as 'entrance creep' and 'exit creep' respectively. The escape tunnel, approximately 30" (762mm) square in section, was 77ft (23.5m) in length. The exit hatch opened near the bank of a small ditch, on the other side of which are the remains of a small OP. Today the exit tunnel, being mostly constructed of corrugated iron and wood has collapsed.

The main bunker according to Claude Varley, whose family farmed there, was blown up by a Royal Engineer unit in 1960, as part of a training exercise.

No surviving members were found for interview.

5.23 Construction drawing of the Hornsea Patrol's OB at Goxhill. (Rev Peter Hollis coll.)

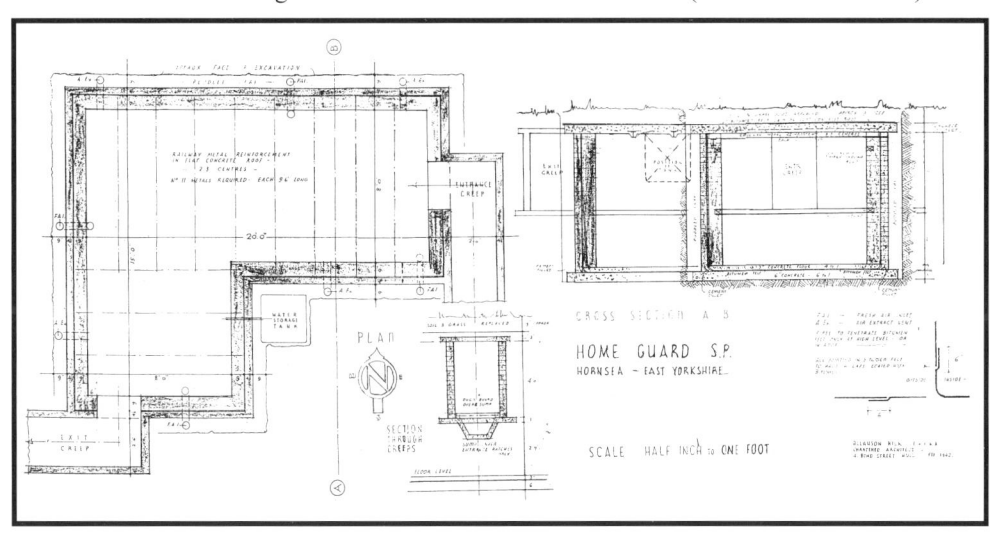

Group No.6, was commanded by Captain Harry Dixon, a farmer from Old Hall, Sunk Island. Harry Dixon was born on 8.6.1905. The Group Sgt. Clerk was Sgt. George Johnson of Halsham, a tractor driver born on 6.8.1905. The Group consisted of the Skeffling, Sunk Island and Withernsea patrols.

Skeffling Patrol

Patrol Members (1944 List)	Civilian Occupation	Date of Birth
Sgt. Henry F Robinson	Farmer	08.11.1902
Cpl Leonard Medforth	Farmer	12.05.1914
Pte. Edward Wilkin	Farmer	17.10.1903
Pte. Robert Pinder	Farm Worker	18.08.1901
Pte. Richard W Dixon	Farmer	06.12.1922
Pte. Arthur O Welton	Fruit Broker	03.05.1905

Pte. Walter Caley, of Burton Pidsea, had been an earlier member of the patrol.

No surviving members of the patrol were found for interview, but Mrs Hodgson, the daughter of the late Edward Wilkin, provided a sketch of the former OB and some details of the patrol.

The OB was located on Winsetts Farm about ½ mile (0.8km) south-east of Skeffling village. The actual site was also about ½ mile north of the Humber bank, and was the nearest OB to the Spurn peninsular.

According to Mrs Hodgson the OB was built under one of two derelict cottages, used by the Humber Coast Guard as a temporary morgue for bodies washed up in the Humber Estuary.

Entrance to the OB was via a trap door hidden under a pile of bricks next to the east wall of the cottage. The chamber, situated under one of the cottage ground floors, was revetted with corrugated iron sheeting. Bunk beds lined two of the walls. There was also a hinged wooden table and an Elsan toilet.

The escape exit consisted of short tunnel with a hatch into the scullery floor of the adjoining cottage.

A telephone line linked the OB with the Winsetts farmhouse which had a clear view of all shipping on the Humber.

Mike Welton, of Easington, whose Uncle Arthur was in the patrol, has revealed a small structure in a drain bank some 600 yds (550m) to the east of the OB. It appears to be an observation post (OP) with stone revetting to the drain bank.

The derelict cottages containing the OB have long since been demolished.

5.25 Skeffling Patrol's OB was under cottages, now demolished between the dyke and roadway in the centre of the photograph. (Author 2000)

5.26 Skeffling Patrol's OP being exposed by Mike Welton, whose Uncle Arthur was a former member. (Author 2000)

5.24 Sketch Drawing of the Skeffling Patrol's OB by Mrs Hodgson, daughter of former patrol member Edward Wilkins. (Author's coll.)

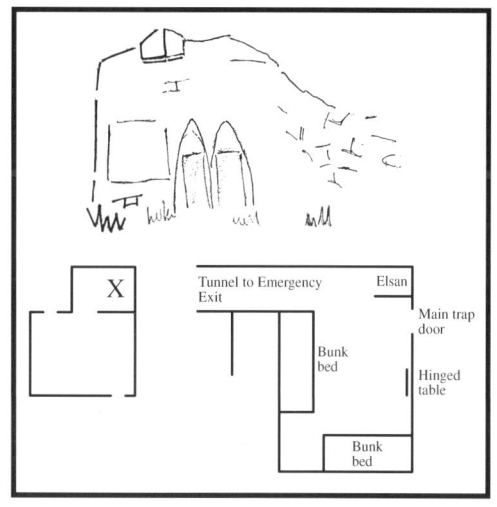

Sunk Island Patrol

Patrol Members (1944 list)	Civilian Occupation	Date of Birth
Sgt John R Wigham	Agricultural Committee Official	1.5.1916
Cpl Charles K Todd	Farmer	28.3.1924
Pte John A Meadley	Farm Worker	14.11.1912
Pte Leonard Harrison	Tractor Driver	6.10.1914
Pte James Carter-Smith	Agricultural Machinery Supt	28.2.1898

Pte Robert H Dixon, of Burstwick, and Pte William Farndale, of Patrington, had both been earlier patrol members. No surviving members have been found for interview but Harry Dixon, the son of the late Captain Dixon, provided helpful information as to the location of the OB. Apparently it had been built into the bank of Spragger Drain about 350 yds (320m) from the Spragger Clough (sluice) on the Humber River. It has been destroyed in recent times by drainage improvement works. Harry Dixon recalled the discovery of a cache of explosives hidden under a bridge at the Old Hall nearby, presumably hidden by his late father at the family farm. No details are available on the OB to determine whether it was a MkI or MkII version.

Withernsea Patrol

Patrol Members (1944 list)	Civilian Occupation	Date of Birth
Sgt William D Farndale	Tractor driver	19.9.1914
Cpl Percival G Hick	Blr. Coverer	8.1.1897
Pte John Gibson	Farmer	16.4.1912
Pte Walter Lowery	Tractor Driver	9.6.1923

Sgt John Thompson, Pte Grassam, Pte Horace Joy, Pte George Conner, Pte Kenneth Perry and Pte Norman Woodcock had been earlier members of the patrol.

Only Pte George Conner was found for interview. They had originally been called an 'Observation Unit' and exercised twice a week, on Wednesday and Saturday. Night training was carried out on Saturdays when they would attack local targets e.g. searchlight batteries. George Conner recalled that during one attack he was hit with a rifle butt, as the defenders did not know who he was. He resigned that very night!

The OB consisted of a simple dugout lined with pit props and corrugated steel. It was built by a Royal Engineer Unit on the top of a hill near Little England Hill Farm. Mr Conner suggested that it was now destroyed, as most MkI types usually are.

5.27 Group No 7 (Beverley North, Beverley South and Walkington patrols) training at Bluestone Quarry, Walkington c1944.
Back Row: N Blake, unknown, C Wright, W Smith, H Lenton.
Middle Row: A Oxtoby, A Meek, D Pattison (?), Capt Carrington Front Row: B Taylor, J Micklethwaite, P Paget. (Mrs A Taylor)

5.28 L.R.Padget, B Taylor, J.Micklethwaite, C Wright, unknown, unknown, A.Oxtoby, A.Meek, H Lenton, G Higgins, Capt Carrington, N Verity, W Smith, - Hanger (?), N.Blake. (Mrs A Taylor)

Group No.7, was commanded by Captain Cyril Carrington of Beverley. Born on 3.12.1899, he was a leather sales manager with the local tannery of W M Hodgson. He was also the Assistant Area Group Commander for the East Riding Southern Area.

The Group Sgt. Clerk was Sgt Herbert Gillyon, a leather worker at the same tannery, born on 25.02.1906.

The Group consisted of the Beverley North, Beverley South, and Walkington patrols. Although the 1944 list shows two Beverley patrols, an earlier Home Guard transfer list suggests that there was possibly only one original patrol. This view is supported by interviews held with the few surviving members and other informants.

For instance Sgt. Charles Sykes was described as a Patrol leader by two surviving members of different Beverley patrols. Also Mr G W Hardy, recalls as a 15 year old acting as messenger boy between Captain Carrington and Sergeant Sykes. Apparently he was replaced at some time by Sgt. Oxtoby and appears in the final 1944 list as a private. Also Pte. Micklethwaite, although officially listed as a member of the Walkington Patrol, is often referred to as a Beverley Patrol member. The past is definitely somewhat hazy and it is understandably difficult for members to recall precise events in a secret organisation over fifty years previously.

Beverley North Patrol

Patrol Members (1944 list)	Civilian Occupation	Date of Birth
Sgt. Charles Wright	Tannery Foreman	14.7.1908
Cpl. William Smith	Baker	21.9.1903
Pte. Horace Lenton	Baker	4.1.1913
Pte. George A Higgins	Valuer	14.2.1901
Pte. Charles P Sykes	Transport Manager	4.2.1901
Pte. Percy Padget	Plater-Ship Building	4.9.1920

The OB was built into the side of a former chalk quarry to the west of Victoria Road, Beverley near Chalk Villa. It was a 'Nissen hut' type (MkII) structure with an entrance tunnel made of concrete culvert pipes. Mr Overton (Beverley) recalls that as a young boy, he and two friends accidentally discovered the entrance whilst sliding down the quarry face. It appeared to be full of ammunition / weapons. They 'liberated' two or three flares which they let off in the quarry.

Former Corporal Bill Smith recalled that their local training was carried out at 'Bluestone Quarry' on Little Weighton Road, Walkington.

Training here was carried out on a Group basis with the Beverley South and Walkington Patrols. He had retained photographs showing the group in training. Mr A W Hardy recalled that transporting the patrols was carried out by a Mr Tattersall (a Wm Hodgson employee) using the firm's transport.

Today the old Victoria Road quarry has been filled in and laid out as a play area. There is no sign of the former OB.

5.29 Charlie Mason on top of Beverley South Patrol OB. The depression in the foreground is the collapsed escape tunnel which entered the OB via the, now exposed, brick end wall. (Author 1995)

5.30 Ardens Vaults, Hengate, Beverley, former meeting place of Beverley Patrol members. (Author 1999)

Beverley South Patrol

Patrol Members (1944 list)	Civilian Occupation	Date of Birth
Sgt. Arthur Oxtoby	Lorry Driver	27.3.1912
Cpl. Norman J Blake	Research Chemist	6.6.1914
Pte. Hampton Lee	Chemist –Leather	3.6.1912
Pte. Arthur Meek	Lorry Driver	23.2.1912
Pte. David A Patterson	Draughtsman – Tool	14.7.1915
Pte. Edward W Shaw	Ship Building – Electric Welder	27.6.1915

Former Cpl. Norman Blake, when interviewed, recalled Pte. Nick Verity had been an earlier patrol member. Apparently the Patrol first met in the cellar of Arden's Vaults next to the White Horse Inn (Nellies) in Hengate. This was chosen by the original patrol leader, Sgt. Charles Sykes, for the reason that a group of men frequenting premises adjoining a public house would not cause undue suspicion. There was probably a better reason – the beer!

Arden's Vaults, a 17th century wine cellar, is nearly 100ft (30.5m) long and 20ft (6m) wide. There is a similar size chamber above. This cellar, with a vaulted brick roof, would have made an ideal 'plotting chamber' for a patrol carrying out clandestine activities. At some stage during the War, it was used as a public air raid shelter with concrete blast walls inserted at either end. These features still exist today as also does the emergency escape hatch into the adjoining public house yard.

Their OB, a MkII Nissen hut structure, was built underground in Johnson's Pit, a woodland to the east of the Walkington to Bentley road. Entrance was via vertical hatch, with an escape tunnel, constructed of timber and corrugated sheeting, dropping down to a small stream.

Although built, as normal, in strict secrecy, it was closely observed by the young members of the 'Bentley Gang' on whose territory it was located. Two members of that gang were the Drew brothers who lived at Jock's Lodge. Colin Drew recalls that they entered the OB and found the bunk beds. The tunnel, which has now collapsed, had a blind off-shoot possibly for storing explosives.

Their unauthorised escapade quickly reached the attention of the authorities in a most unusual way. Apparently their schoolmaster at the Walkington Village School had suggested that, as part of the English composition lessons, they should write letters to someone living away. Colin's brother Redvers decided to write a letter to his Uncle Walt, who was in a German prisoner of war camp. In his letter he described their discovery of the secret bunker.

Fortunately, the letter was intercepted by either their schoolmaster, Beth Taylor or the official censor, possibly the former, as he was by chance the leader of the Walkington Auxiliary Unit Patrol. The boys were ultimately called out in front of the class for a verbal dressing down by the local policeman. Happily the enemy remained unaware of the Secret Army activities.

Even today the OB's true identity remains a secret, as it is always referred to as a 'ammunition or bomb' store in connection with a nearby former AA gun site.

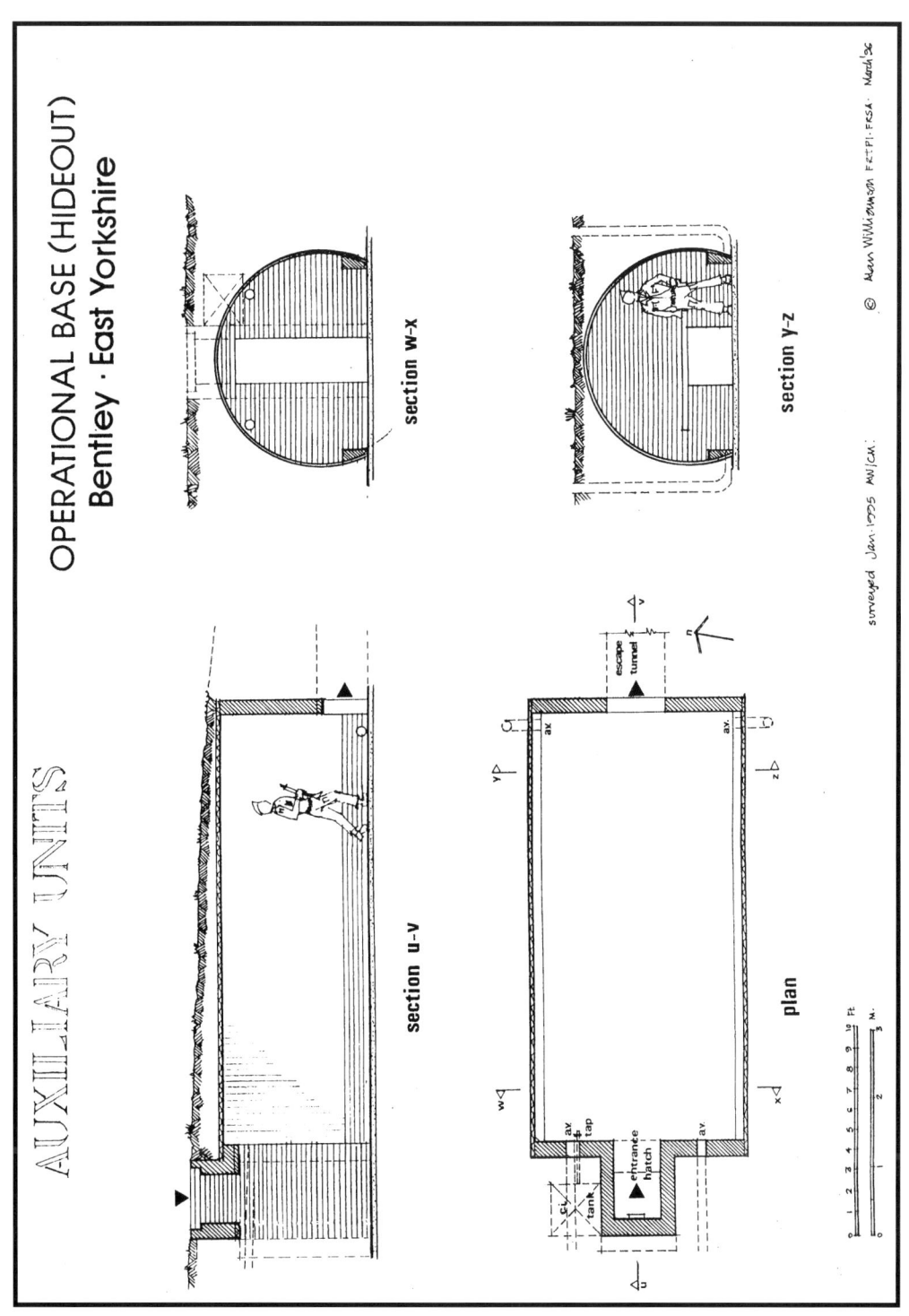

5.31 Survey drawing of Beverley South Patrol OB near Bentley. (Author)

Walkington Patrol

Patrol Members (1944 list)	Civilian Occupation	Date of Birth
Sgt. Bethel Taylor	School Master	20.11.1909
Cpl. Eric Jackson	Farmer	1.2.1915
Pte. Jesse Micklethwaite	Engineer	17.3.1905
Pte. Peter T Birkhead	Draughtsman	25.1.1920
Pte. Edward Hanger	Paint Manufacturer	7.7.1905
Pte. John Hanger	Paint Manufacturer	10.10.1913

The patrol's first OB was a simple dug out or MkI version, located into a former chalk pit at the junction of crossroads at Walkington Wold.

Like many other MkI OBs it was considered to be too close to the road junction which possibly led to its early discovery. A new MkIII version was built by the Royal Engineers on Crawberry Hill nearer to Bishop Burton.

According to Ernie Ellerington, on whose father's land it was built, a nearby field was used as a mortar firing range. Against the background noise of this range, the sound of explosives used to blast a hole for OB, would have gone unnoticed. Possibly the mortar range was only used as cover for the building operations. However, the tail fins of mortar bombs are occasionally discovered during ploughing operations.

The OB was built much deeper than normal, with its floor level about 12ft (3.6m) below ground level. Concrete blocks were used instead of bricks, and the entrance had built-in steps formed from 2" piping.

At either end were small vestibules created by the use of concrete blast walls. The tunnel escape, made out of 30" (76mm) concrete pipes, was about 14ft (4.2) in length and had a right angle bend about halfway.

Ernie Ellerington recalled that it had a central folding table as well as bunk beds. Shelves still exist in the two vestibules. Mrs A Taylor, Sgt. Beth Taylor's widow had somehow known about the OB in Crawberry Hill, and her husband had, dutifully reported this fact to the Intelligence Officer, Captain Leigh-Lye.

Training was carried out with the Beverley patrols at Bluestone Quarry and another pit close to Bishop Burton.

Today the OB still exists, although the central section has collapsed due to rusting of the roof vent and the heavy weight of the chalk overburden. The entrance shaft and escape tunnels are still intact.

Its existence was first revealed in 1992 by local farmer, John Dunning in his book on Bishop Burton entitled 'Bishop Burton and its People.'

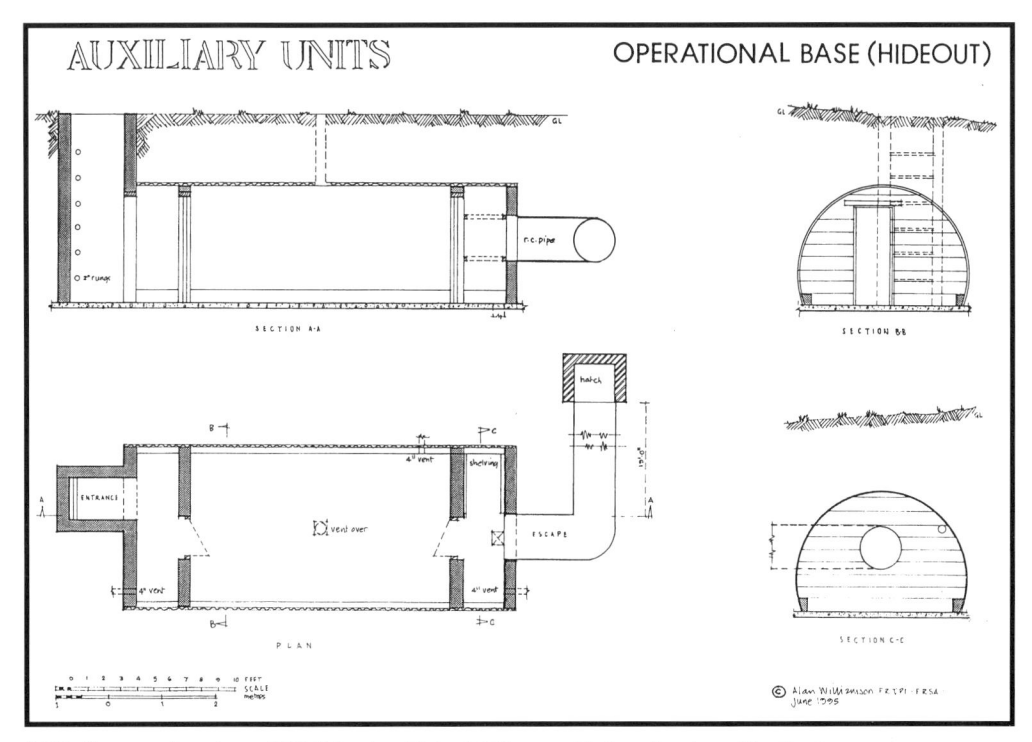

5.32 Survey drawing of Walkington Patrol OB near Bishop Burton. (Author)

5.33 Interior of Walkington Patrol OB showing escape tunnel entrance. (Author 1995)

5.34 Charlie Mason 'escaping' in the Walkington Patrol OB concrete tunnel. (Author 1995)

71

Group No.8, was commanded by Captain Stanley Holmes, a Cottingham provision merchant, born on 10.4.1896. The Group Sergeant was Sgt Robert E Williams of Hull, born on 12.05.1901. His civilian occupation was as a Foreman. He had originally been a member of the South Cave Patrol when he had lived in that area.

The Group consisted of Bilton, Cottingham North and Cottingham South patrols.

Bilton Patrol

Patrol Members (1944 list)	Civilian Occupation	Date of Birth
Sgt Frank Jameson	Ship's Plumber	20.02.1895
Cpl. John H Holley	Stone worker	04.02.1905
Pte Albert Carr	Market Gardener	05.06.1913
Pte Albert H Grantham	Farm worker	18.07.1913
Pte Frank W Jubb	Ship's Joiner	29.04.1909

Another member of the patrol had been Pte Sydney Jameson, who was discharged due to his hand being severely damaged during a hand grenade training exercise.

The OB was built into the north bank of the Thirtleby and Wyton Drain, about 150 yds (137m) to the west of Langdale Lane, Ganstead. From contemporary accounts it appeared to be a MkI type structure. Clive Holley remembers being taken into the bunker by his father soon after the end of the war. He has kindly drawn, from memory, the details of the layout and equipment. This is an excellent representation of a standard OB, and although not to scale, is remarkably accurate. Today there is only a small depression in the ground, the OB having been destroyed by either drainage works or the creation of the adjoining golf course.

According to Trevor Holley, Clive's brother, the patrol's training was either done at their respective homes or at Burton Constable Park. Mrs Jasmine Mires of Burton Constable, recalled that her late father Robert Thirsk was involved with some 'Home Guard' activities in the woods. Robert Thirsk, a World War I veteran, was the Estate Game Keeper during the Second World War.

Trevor Holley still has his father's 1942 Military Engineering Manual relating to demolitions. It was apparently issued to Lt Holmes (later captain), whose name appears on the front cover, and became the Group Commander.

Cottingham North Patrol

Patrol Members (1944 list)	Civilian Occupation	Date of Birth
Sgt Jack H Steel	Sanitary Inspector	10.09.1908
Cpl Joseph Long	Grocer	17.07.1897
Pte John G Lindsay	Doctor – GP	
Pte Ronald Newlove	Fitter	19.11.1926
Pte Mark K Wilson	Market Gardener	04.12.1913
Pte Alan Bolton	Farmer	25.12.1926
Pte John S Rhodes	Butcher	24.06.1913

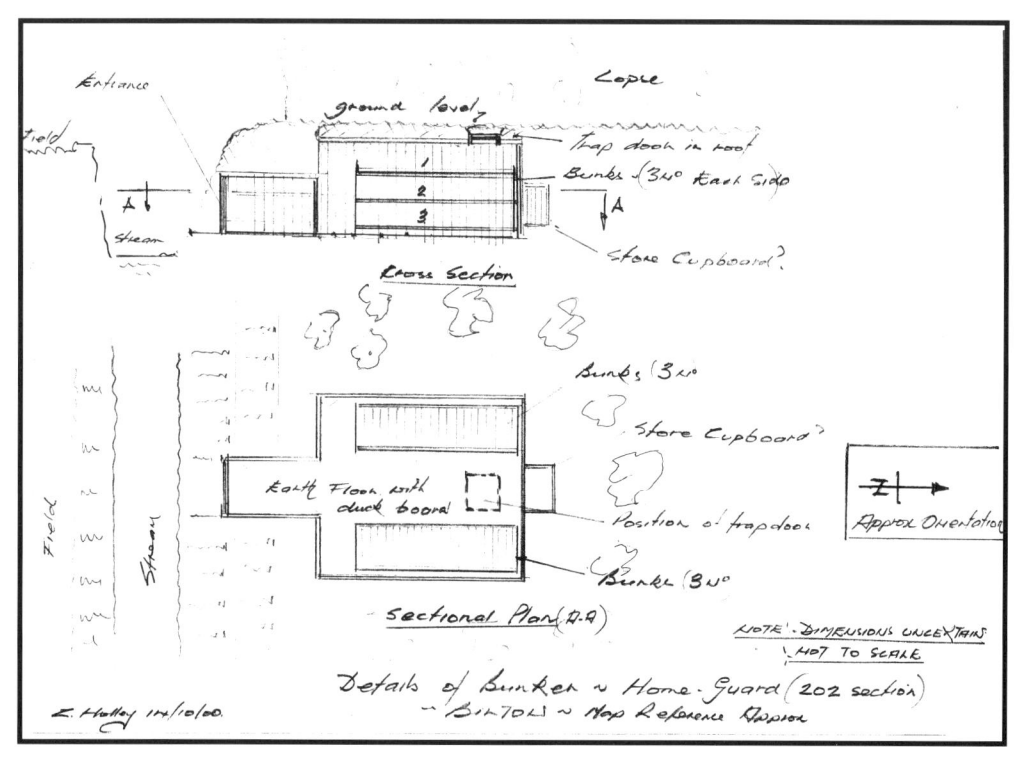

5.35 Sketch Drawing of the former Bilton Patrol OB by Clive Holley, son of Patrol member John Holley. (Clive Holley)

5.36 Trevor Holley, Clive's Brother, at the site of the former Bilton Patrol OB. (Author 1999)

Other original members had been Cpl Harry Nicholson, Pte Leonard Wollas, Pte Reginald Hoggins and Pte H Brocklehurst. Harry Nicholson had left the patrol to join the SAS, where apparently he was made sergeant within three weeks. This rapid promotion was due to his actions in preventing theft of highly important equipment about to be parachuted to the SAS secretly operating in occupied France.

Leonard Wollas left in 1943 to join the army and served in the Middle East with the Sudan Defence Force.

According to the Group Commander, Captain Holmes, in an interview for the Yorkshire Evening Post in 1968, the OB was at Harland Rise, to the north of Cottingham, but had been destroyed. He recalled that it was beneath a greenhouse and '*to get into it you went down to the boilerhouse and moved aside a pile of coke*'.

Mrs Susan Pace, remembers her father, the late Leonard Wollas, taking her after the war to see the site of the greenhouse and adjoining house, which was called the Grange. Apparently this was demolished as part of the Harland Way new school development. Her father also told her about the patrol nearly being wiped out by fumes from the boilerhouse. Fortunately patrol member Doctor Lindsey, who had been called out to an emergency, returned just in time to find his comrades on the point of death. She also had a lucky escape herself, when a bullet narrowly missed her when her father was cleaning his unloaded (!) pistol. The bullet remained embedded in the skirting board until their home was demolished in 1963.

No information is available on the size and construction of the OB, although Captain Holmes had stated that they were built by the Royal Engineers, and usually lined with corrugated iron or bricks.

Cottingham South Patrol

Patrol Members (1944 list)	Civilian Occupation	Date of Birth
Sgt George E Bolder	Dairy Manager	04.03.1896
Cpl John N Nunn	Clerk	09.04.1908
Pte William Kettley	Warehouseman	07.08.1897

Cpl Arthur Singleton, Pte Cecil Osborne, Pte Thomas Holmes, and Pte Frederick Paddison were earlier members of the Patrol.

The OB appears to have been in the old chalk caves in the grounds of Castle Hill Hospital. These caves, on the east side of Cottingham to Beverley Road were the result of quarrying in the early part of 19th century to provide foundation material for the Cottingham Castle, a mansion later burnt down in 1869.

Some eyewitness accounts recall seeing a OB type structure exposed to view soon after the end of the War. Unfortunately this quarry area has since been filled with waste material, and today no signs of the OB remain.

However two observation posts (OPs) have been discovered, some 98 yds (90m) to the east, on the edge of a small plantation. One was underground and the other in a nearby mature beech tree.

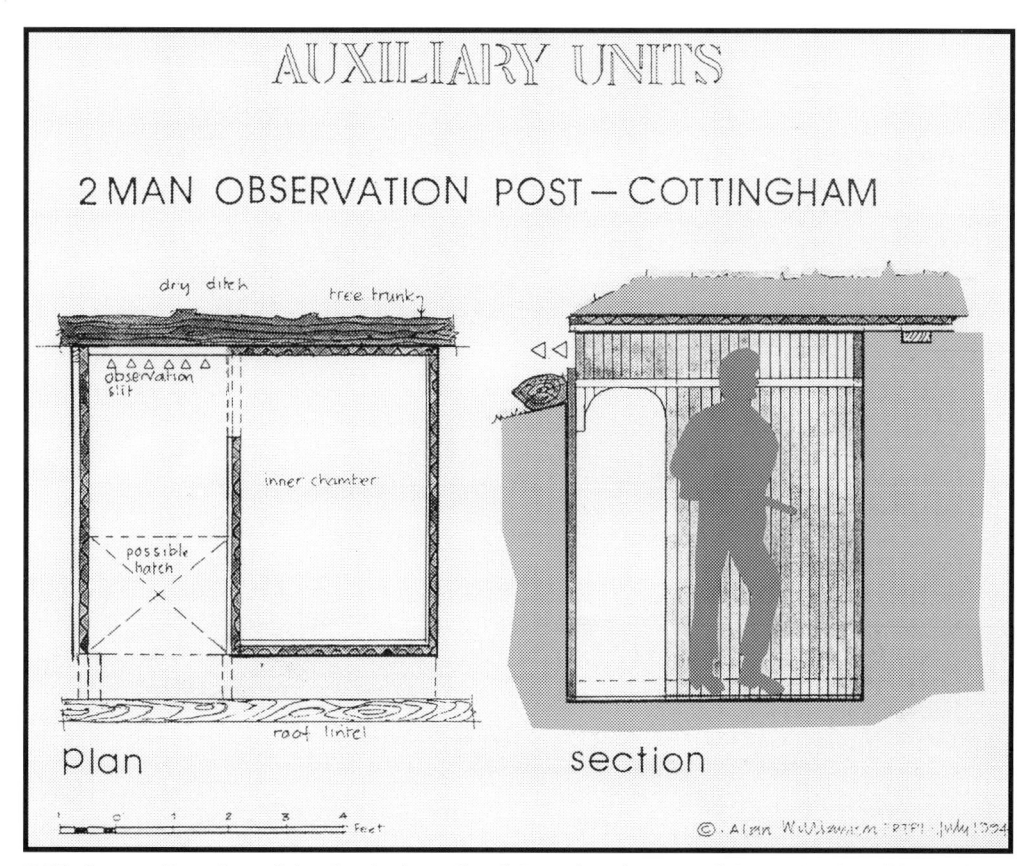

5.37 Survey Drawing of the Cottingham South Patrol underground OP at Castle Hill. (Author)

5.38 Excavation and recording of Cottingham South Patrol OP. (Author)

5.39 Peter Emerton demonstrating the Cottingham South Patrol's high level OP situated in a mature beech tree at Castle Hill (the tree has since been felled). (Author 1994)

The underground OP had been partially destroyed by the tipping of waste material, but a careful excavation, with co-operation of the hospital authority, revealed a structure, approximately 6' 0" (1.8m) square by 6' 6" (1.98m) deep. The walls were revetted with corrugated steel sheeting held in place by salvaged timber. The roof had been of similar construction. Internally it was divided into two equal compartments, one of which had an observation loophole, overlooking the Eppleworth Road. It was of sufficient size to accommodate two men, one watching and the other resting.

The tree OP had metal rods and angle iron deeply embedded in the trunk to assist climbing. A cleft in the tree was sufficiently large enough to practically conceal an observer. Confirmation of this tree OP was given by Captain Holmes in his 1968 interview with Yorkshire Evening Post. Unfortunately this tree has now been felled by hospital authority on the grounds of safety.

No surviving members of this patrol were found for interview.

5.40 Cottingham North Patrol. Note seated member with 'Tommy Gun.' Leonard Wollas is third from left and Harry Nicholson (with commando knife) is fourth left. (Mrs Susan Pace coll.)

Group No.9, was commanded by Lieut. William Cross, an agricultural worker born on 1.1.1903. The Assistant Group Commander was 2nd Lieut. James Harrop, an Aircraft Draughtsman, born on 19.7.1914. The Group Sgt Clerk, was Sgt. John Cross, an Accounts Clerk, born on 17.5.1904.

The group consisted of the Brough, North Cave and South Cave patrols.

Brough Patrol

Patrol Members (1944 list)	Civilian Occupation	Date of Birth
Sgt. Alan R Scott	Aircraft Draughtsman	6.2.1903
Pte. Robert H Adie	Aircraft Draughtsman	30.9.1911
Pte. William D Beveridge	Aircraft Draughtsman	5.1.1910
Pte. Thomas C Campbell	Aircraft Draughtsman	11.8.1899
Pte. Stephen C Woodward	Aircraft Draughtsman	30.4.1902

The earlier members of the patrol were Pte. Ronald Massey, and Pte. Alec Jeffrey. Pte. Massey, an aircraft stress analyst, born on 11.2.1916 was later a sergeant in charge of the South Cave Patrol. No former members have been found for interview, and therefore much reliance has been placed on information obtained from surviving members of the other patrols in the group.

The first OB, a MkI dugout was thought to have been located in Stockbridge Plantations at the junction of the Cave Road with Stockbridge Lane. This area has been subject to development, and no evidence of the OB's survival has been found.

It has also been suggested that an underground structure had been found in a former quarry, known as the Cockle Pits, further to the north east of Brough.

Despite extensive searches of this former quarry, which has been the subject of random tipping over the years, no trace of any identifiable structure was found.

However, it is established that a new OB was built in Dale Plantation at Welton Dale, to the north of Welton village.

Information on this location came about in a most interesting manner. Cyril Widd, who was born in Welton, was serving with a Guards Regiment in Italy during World War II. One night, during a lull in the battle, he fell into conversation with a American soldier; Cyril, having been asked where he came from in England, naturally said Yorkshire, hoping that someone from the USA may have heard of it. The American said that he had been stationed in Yorkshire, at a small village called Welton, Cyril's home village! Apparently this soldier had been billeted at the local public house, the Green Dragon, and together with his unit, had been building a secret underground bunker in Welton Dale. This later transpired to be the Brough Patrol OB, knowledge of which Cyril Widd was delighted to pass on some 50 years later.

Cyril, a former East Riding Police Sergeant, was of immense help in pointing out this OB and others at Rise and Cottingham. The OB, which appears to have been a MkII Nissan type structure has long since been destroyed and today consists of a series of depressions, which together are about 40ft (12 m) in length. Possibly half the length may relate to a collapsed tunnel. Evidence of corrugated steel sheeting and brickwork show in places. Three local men recall as young Army Cadets, at the end of the War, being shown inside by Lieut. Harrop, prior to demolition.

Some 65ft (21m) to the east of the OB is a further 8ft (2.4m) square dugout. This has natural chalk sides, with remains of some flat corrugated steel sheeting carried on timber supports, still embedded in the overburden at roof level. Being rather large for an OP and appearing to have been quite shallow, it may have had use as separate explosive store for the OB.

At the southern end of Common Lane, Welton where it meets the Humber bank, is a small group of trees, one of which may have been used as an OP. This particular old Ash tree has twelve 12" (30°mm) 'dog spikes' driven into the trunk to form steps. These type of spikes were commonly used in military field engineering, and have been used in OBs. This OP may have been simply an ordinary Home Guard post or used specifically by the Brough patrol.

Further to the north, where Common Lane meets the track of Ings Lane, is another possible OP. Alongside the track, immediately north of Oak Plantation is a structure concealed in the bottom of the ditch. It is made out of half round corrugated sheeting, and very much resembles the OP at Bewholme. Once again its former occupants are unknown.

The Brough Patrol was strategically placed for controlling the major roads and railway line out of Hull, as well as observing river traffic on the Humber. With virtually all of the patrol members employed at the Brough aircraft factory, their intimate knowledge of the adjoining airfield would have been of particular use had it been occupied by enemy forces.

5.41 Charlie Mason pointing to the 'dog spike' steps on an Observation Post tree, overlooking the River Humber, near Welton. (Author 1999)

AUXILIARY UNITS

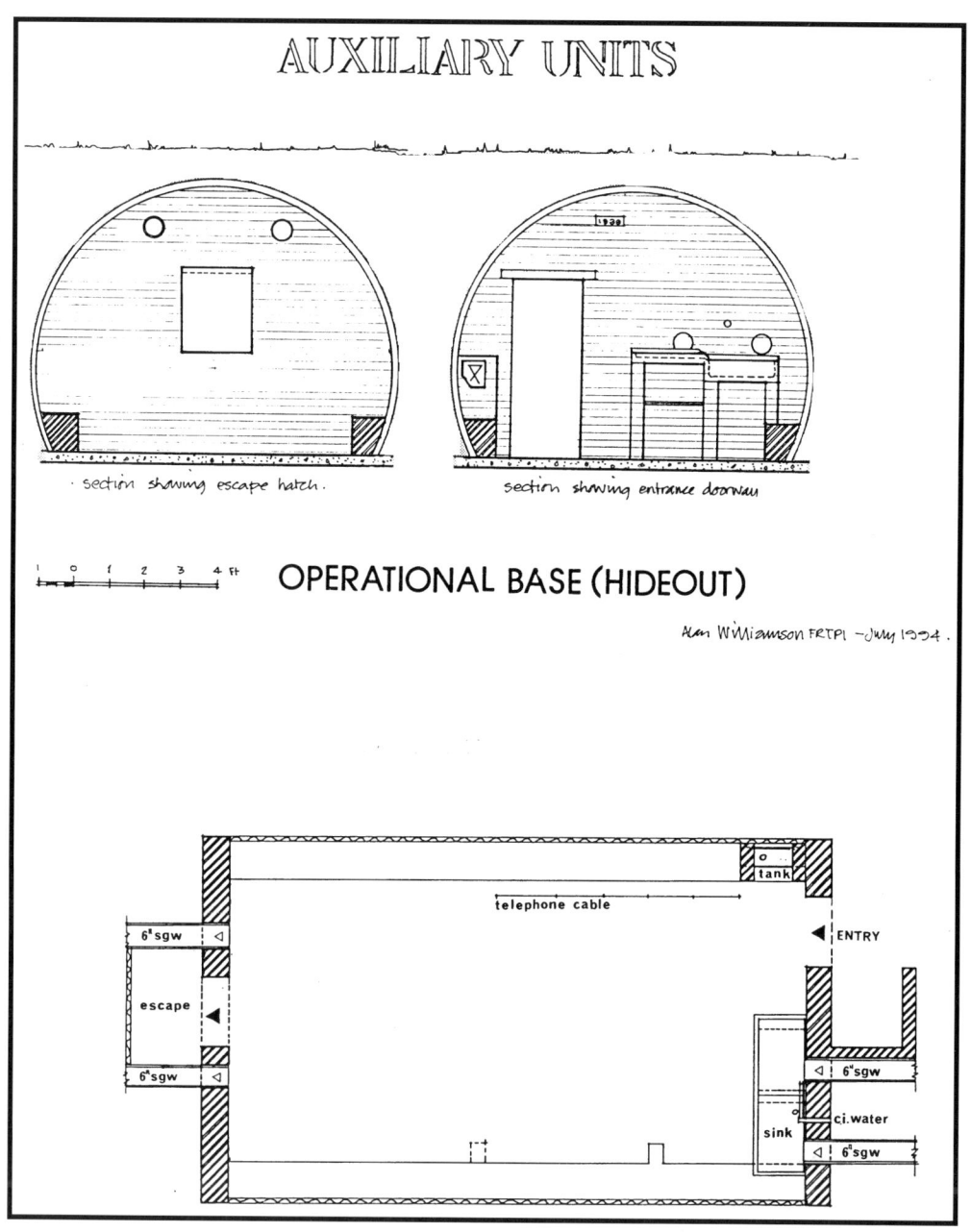

section showing escape hatch. *section showing entrance doorway*

OPERATIONAL BASE (HIDEOUT)

Alan Williamson FRTPI – July 1994.

5.42 1994 Survey drawing of North Cave Patrol OB. (Author)

5.43 Charlie Mason inspecting the partially destroyed roof of the North Cave Patrol MkI OB. (Author 1994)

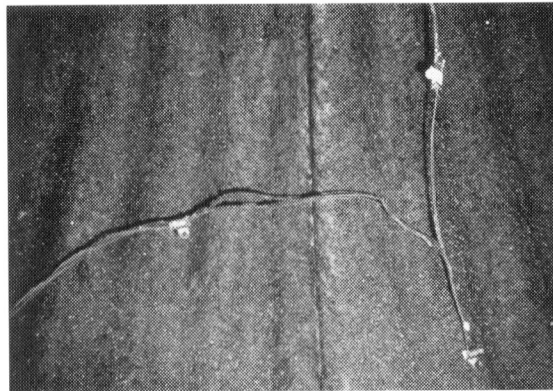

5.44 Telephone wire, originally linking North Cave Patrol OB with the OP, still fastened to the OB roof. (Author 1994)

5.46 North Cave Patrol OB's customised sink and drainer unit. Note fresh inlet pipe at the rear, and C.I water pipe inlet. (Author 1994)

5.45 The strange date '1939' applied in raised 'cement slip' lettering to an internal wall of the North Cave MkII OB. Note the OB was not built until 1941 at the earliest! (Author 1994)

North Cave Patrol

Patrol Members (1944 list)	Civilian Occupation	Date of Birth
Sgt. Harold Cobb	Aircraft Fitter	2.10.1919
Pte. Kenneth Thornham	Tractor Driver	14.1.1913
Pte. Edgar Cobb	Aircraft Woodworker	20.12.1912
Pte. Duncan Suddaby	Aircraft Fitter	20.4.1914
Pte. Bernard Thompson	Bricklayer	21.11.1916

Other earlier members of the patrol were, Sgt. Frank Lowthorpe (a bricklayer born on 14.6.1904). Pte. Arthur Jackson (aircraft fitter born on 22.2.1925), and Pte. Cyril Pease.

Two former members of the patrol, Duncan Suddaby and Arthur Jackson were located for interview.

The original OB, a MkI type dugout was built in Stonepit plantation, halfway between Hotham village and the South Cave to Newbald road (A 1034). This was ultimately replaced with a nearby MkII Nissen type structure. The MkI, roofed with half round, steel corrugated sheeting, was retained as the main store for explosives and ammunition. They were linked by a tunnel, lined and roofed with flat corrugated steel sheeting. Entrance to the MkII OB was via a hatch into the MkI OB. The hatch was concealed by a hollow tree stump, which could be removed by sliding action. The escape hatch was surprisingly close to the entrance hatch.

The OB contained a table, seating and two double bunk beds. The advantage of having bricklayers in the patrol is shown by the customised brick sink unit and fuel store.

What is of particular interest is the date '1939' written in applied mortar slip over the entrance doorway. The significance of the date is strange, in that the OB was not built until 1941 at the earliest. There is other similar applied writing nearby, but now completely illegible. One can only presume that 1939 relates to the outbreak of the War.

The OB was linked to an OP built nearby in the eastern boundary of the plantation, with good views of any movement on the main roads coming from High Hunsley Hill.

Today the OB is still intact, although the original tunnel access has collapsed. The roof of the MkI OB still survives, but may have been partially demolished or infilled with earth material. The OB still retains the special sink unit and fuel storage container. Attached to the roof is a 6ft (1.8) length of the original telephone cable that linked the OB with the nearby OP.

A small depression in the ground, on the eastern boundary, still identifies the original OP.

From memory, Arthur Jackson, a retired hotelier from Windsor, has drawn an excellent sketch of the two OB's and their relationship with the OP.

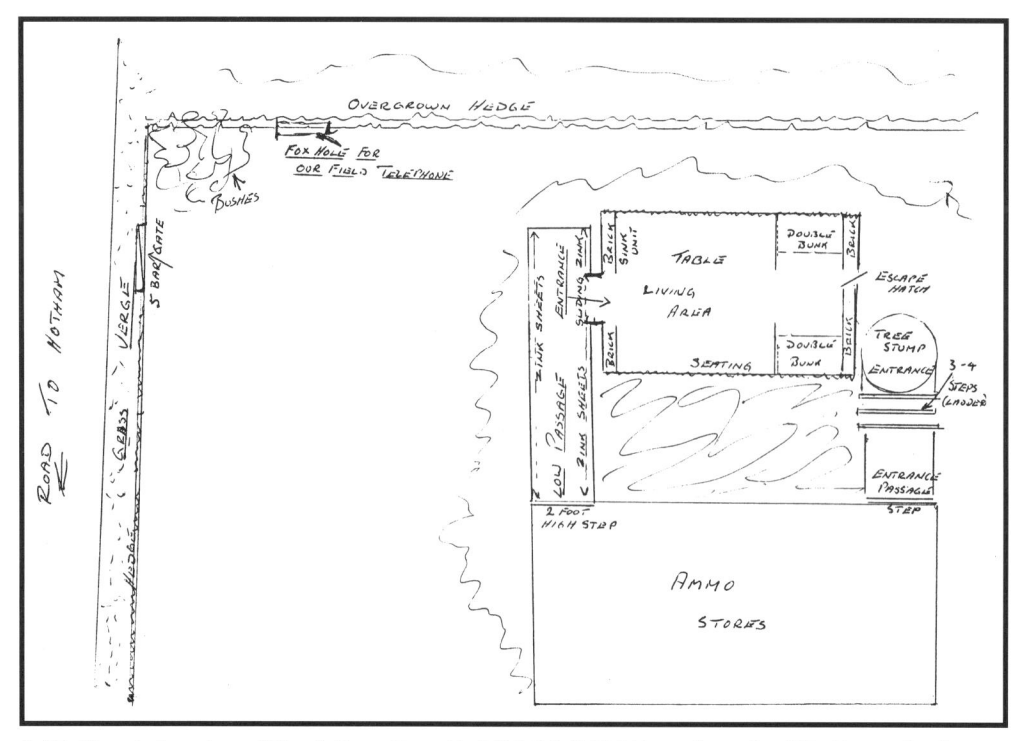

5.47 Sketch drawing of North Cave Patrol's MkI & MkII OBs and nearby OP. Drawn by former member Arthur Jackson. The 'Ammo Store' was the original MkI OB. (Arthur Jackson)

5.48 Arthur Jackson, a former member of the North Cave Patrol. (Author 2000)

South Cave Patrol

Patrol Members (1944 list)	**Civilian Occupation**	**Date of Birth**
Sgt Ronald S Massey	Aircraft-stress analyst	11.2.1916
Cpl Benjamin R Taylor	Timber Feller	25.3.1918
Pte Gordon P Watson	Technical Author	21.8.1906
Pte Ernest C Colbeck	Stores Superintendent	1.6.1901
Pte Charles A Mason	Aircraft Engineer	20.2.1914

Earlier members of the patrol had been Sgt Robert E Williams (who became No 8 Group Sgt. Clerk), Cpl John L Cross (who became No9 Group Sgt.Clerk), Pte Stephen C Woodward (aircraft draughtsman), and Pte Thomas S Watson.

Charlie Mason recalls how he was recruited:-

"One day I was walking down the village, and someone spoke to me from behind. I turned round and it was an old friend (Jack Cross). He said that he wanted a word with me. I said what is it about? He replied that it was too hush-hush and that we should go somewhere more quiet.

We sat on the village beck bridge, and he started to tell me a little about an underground army, and was I interested? I said tell me more about it, he couldn't because it was so secret. He said "unless you agree to join is I cannot tell you any more".

So I said that I would think about it. To which he replied "you haven't got time to think about it. There is a meeting tonight and I want to know now!"

I asked him how many others he had got? He said they needed seven, had six and needed me. I asked where he had got the other six from, and he said that they had been picked from the Home Guard. So I said why didn't he get another from the Home Guard? He replied they wanted me because of my background. What background? I asked, to which he simply replied "Out in the woods at night – bang! bang!"

Then it dawned on me – we were a big family, there were six lads and we all liked to do a bit of poaching! We all had guns so it was just natural for us to work in the woods, and I probably knew the area better than the other six members – so I decided to join. We had our first meeting that night, and after much discussion I signed some secret documents.

The first OB, a MkI dugout, was on the western edge of Little Wold Plantation, overlooking the South Cave to Market Weighton road. According to Charlie Mason, it was about 8ft (2.4m) square, with vertical corrugated steel sheets to the sides, concrete pavers for the floor, and covered over with 3-4ft (0.9-1.2m) of earth.

Apparently the patrol occupied their OB for about 2 months until a new MkII OB was built in nearby Drewton Dale at Weedley Springs. This was a MkII Nissen hut type with a vertical entrance and an escape tunnel.

One particular innovation was a flat, wooden trolley, running on castors (furniture wheels) and pulled by ropes at either end. This enabled both heavy supplies, and patrol members to access the OB via the 20-30ft (6m-9m) escape tunnel. This mechanism seems very similar to that portrayed

5.49 Charlie Mason pointing to the roof of the destroyed South Cave Patrol OB. (Author)

5.50 Part of the entrance wooden ladder to the South Cave Patrol OB, exposed by recent subsidence. (Catherine Mason)

5.51 No 9 Group Auxiliary Unit members. Back Row: S Woodward, R Massey, Unknown. Front Row: Unknown, R Williams. (Mrs S Heathcote)

in the classic film "The Great Escape", the story of Allied prisoners of war in occupied Europe.

The use of an escape tunnel for both ingress and egress is not unusual, as it often prevented disturbing carefully landscaped and concealed entrance hatches.

The location of this new OB, almost alongside the former Hull to Barnsley railway line, was strategically placed to control the mile (1.6km) long, deep Drewton tunnel. This could be quickly blocked by explosive charges detonated in one of the many large, brick, overhead airshafts. There were also two nearby shorter tunnels.

Today, the evidence of the OB, which was destroyed after the war, is a large depression containing mangled corrugated sheeting, much chalk overburden and the remains of the end brick walls. More recently, possibly due to subsidence, the top shafts of the original entrance ladder have started to appear.

Built in the steep northern side of Drewton Dale, a single strand of rusty barbed wire, stapled to trees, marks the southern proximity of the OB. The rusty wire, appears to be of World War II vintage, and is a feature, sometimes encountered elsewhere, as in the case of the Crawberry Wood OB at Bishop Burton.

Its purpose could have been twofold, either to prevent unauthorised stumbling on to the OB, or as a simple guideline for the patrol members to locate the OB in the darkness. It should be re-iterated that their perfect camouflage made finding them extremely difficult even during daylight hours. A single strand of wire would not draw undue attention in wartime.

The patrol's equipment consisted of .38 revolvers, a .22 sniper rifle, commando knives, and Sten guns. They had also, earlier, been issued with a Tommy Gun. Charlie Mason also recalled that he had a garrotte or 'cheese cutter', a much more silent way of killing. For training and operations they wore denim uniform, black berets, and rubber agricultural boots.

This equipment was in addition to their normal supply of explosives and demolition packs.

Training was carried out at Middleton on the Wolds HQ, and in nearby woods and quarries.

A typical training programme for the month of February 1944 is shown in the appendices. It is interesting to note that the meeting scheduled for Gordon Watson's house, depended on the agreement of Mrs Watson!

Charlie recalls one major exercise they were involved in with many other Auxiliary Unit patrols:-

I remember one such exercise – we had to attack the Regular Army near Dalton Holme. There were quite a lot of troops, as well as a number of vehicles. Apparently there was more than one Auxiliary Unit patrol involved, in fact quite a number…. It was a long operation. We had flashbombs with time pencils. We marked various vehicles we had been in, and as we came out we also threw flashbombs… everybody was doing it at the same time… they were being attacked from all sides. There was so much going on, so many explosions going on, that we later found out from our Commanding Officer that the Police had been notified – they thought that there had been some sort of enemy landing in that area. Somebody had made a mistake in not notifying the authorities about the exercise."

In the same exercise, Ben Taylor, the only other surviving patrol member, recalled his particular adventure. Having successfully withdrawn, he decided to return to a nearby village to visit friends. He was still wearing his uniform, bearing no insignia, and with a still blacked up face. Carrying no identification papers, he was arrested by the army, and taken locally for questioning. Refusing to answer questions he was to be taken to York for proper interrogation, but was fortunately spotted by an officer, who had been an official umpire on the earlier exercise. He was then thankfully released.

Charlie Mason also recalls the 'awkward' gamekeeper who initially refused his orders to keep away from the area containing the OB. On, reluctantly, leaving he told Charlie he 'knew what was going on down there'. Having officially reported these facts, the patrol had a discussion what to do about the gamekeeper knowing their secret, they decided,

'That when invasion comes, not if it comes, to get rid of him (the gamekeeper), to eliminate him, to boobytrap him, certainly to eliminate him! We would eliminate anyone who threatened our existence, put our hide or existence in jeopardy.'

Later on in the War they volunteered to guard the Isle of Wight at the time of the D-Day Landings. Having got as far as Paragon Station, Hull, they were turned back as no longer required due to the success of the Allied invasion.

However, whilst German invasion became less and less likely, there was always a thought that Hitler could mount diversionary paratroop raids on this country. With this in mind the role of the South Cave patrol was changed to that of an Observation Unit, liaising with the South Cave Home Guard troops. Ben King had retained a copy of the new instructions, which contains a suggestion that the Home Guard and the Patrol should familiarise with each other to avoid any unfortunate accidents! (see Appendix A)

After the stand down, they held just one re-union, that being at the Black Horse public house in nearby Ellerker.

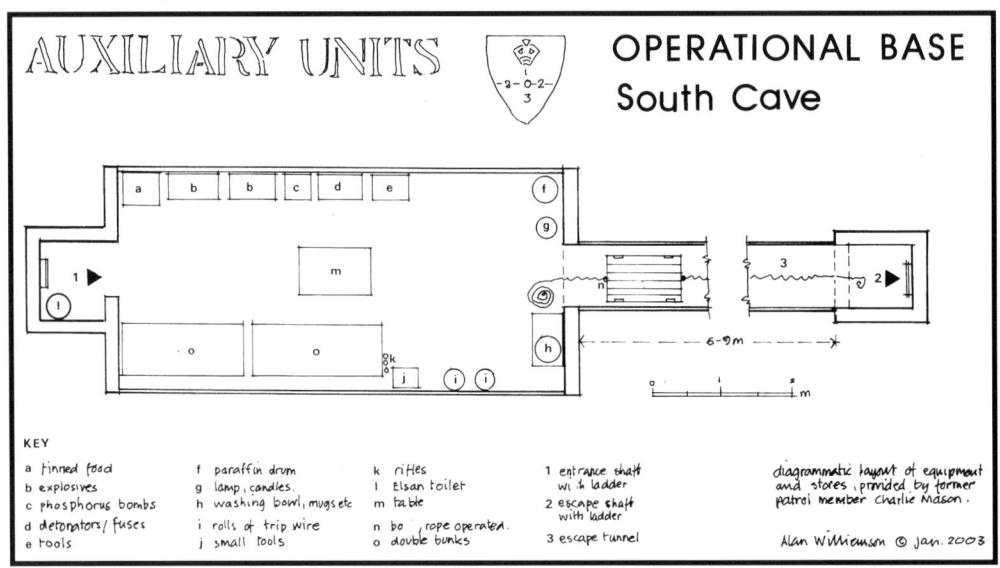

5.52 Sketch layout of the former South Cave Patrol OB. (Author)

5.3 The Lost Patrol

In February 1998, the Yorkshire Post published an article on research being carried out for this very book.

Shock! Horror! Out of the blue came a letter from Ed Maltby, a retired local government officer living at Haxby, near York, saying that he had been a member of a previously unknown patrol. Upto that stage all the East Riding patrols had more or less been accounted for, all being within 20 mile (32km) radius of the coast. According to Ed, his patrol had been much further inland, some 30 miles (48km) from the coast. This patrol, known as the Spaldington Patrol, had operated in complete isolation of the other East Riding patrols, and reported direct to the County Intelligence Officer, Captain Peter Hollis.

Furthermore, it appeared to have been disbanded prior to 1944, as no mention is made in the official list. Ed Maltby was the last surviving member, and without his letter, all knowledge of this patrol would most certainly have been lost.

Ed Maltby joined the patrol in 1940 but was called up for service with the Regular Army in 1941. However, within nine days he was quickly transferred to the Reserve for security reasons. His membership of the Auxiliary Units prompted this decision, in case either careless talk or by capture, the enemy may have stumbled on knowledge of the secret resistance army.

He was eventually called up again in 1943, together with other Auxiliary Unit members from the East Coast and South Wales.

After training and posting to other units, they were all called together again, and asked to volunteer for service with the SAS. At one stage Lord Lovat sought them out for his famous commando unit, the Lovat Scouts. On joining the SAS he met Sgt. Harry Nicholson, a former member of the Cottingham North Patrol. Ed also recalls two senior SAS officers who were responsible for forming the Kent XII Corps Observation Unit, thought to be the first County Auxiliary Unit, and prototype for the rest of the country. They were Col. Peter Fleming (brother of James Bond creator, Ian Fleming) and Captain 'Mad' Mike Calvert.

In 1945, Ed and his unit were dispatched to Norway to 'encourage' the German army to speed up its surrender and disarmament.

The finding of Ed Maltby, and a chance remark to Mrs Susan Pace (daughter of the late Leonard Woollas, Cottingham North Patrol) led to her husband, Tony, finding a long lost distant cousin, the very same Ed Maltby!

Spaldington Patrol

Patrol Members	Civilian Occupation	No Information on Age
Sgt. John Morrison	Farmer	
Cpl. Steve Rennie	Farmer	
Pte. Ed Maltby	Grocer	
Pte. Jack J Fitzgerald	Farm Foreman	
Pte. Cyril Hessle	Ex. Farmer (Captain World War I)	
Pte. Bob Roper	Poultry Farmer (?) (A wrestler from Cumberland)	
Pte. Sam Suttle	Labourer (ex. Regular Army)	
Pte. Hill	Poultry Farmer (?)	

A Pte. Harold Hargrove was an earlier member of the patrol. Both Pte. Roper and Pte Hill left the patrol for reasons of ill health.

Their OB was the only one in the East Riding and possibly the whole country, which was actually built above ground, and not underground. A previous attempt had been made to build an underground structure but was abandoned due to high water levels in the area.

To the north-east of Spaldington village was an old mill house, no longer in use. Inside this a Nissen hut type structure was built on the ground floor, with a strong brick retaining wall alongside. Outside the mill building a large demolition charge was detonated, with the resulting blast causing the building to collapse and cover the Nissen hut OB. The explosion caused a large bomb-like crater outside, and the locals were told that a stray German bomb had hit the mill, a ploy often used elsewhere to disguise covert building operations.

A tunnel access, under the brick rubble was made into the OB, and a underground tunnel into an adjoining grassfield provided the escape. This latter tunnel had a grass covered trapdoor exit.

Ventilation was provided to the OB by the 8ft (2.4m) high stump of the mill house chimney, which was also wide enough to act as the observation post (OP)

For security reasons the OB was little used, with meetings taking place in the saddle-room at Willitoft Hall, about 1 mile (1.6km) to the north west.

Ed Maltby recalled that Sgt. Morrison went to Coleshill for training, whilst the rest of the patrol were trained at Middleton Hall. They also received special instruction at the Blackburn aircraft factory at Brough on aeroplane sabotage, as the nearby Breighton RAF airfield would have been one of their principal targets.

Their equipment consisted of the usual Tommy Gun; 303 rifle and a .22 sniper rifle. Individually they all had Smith & Wesson revolvers and a truncheon. Unusually, according to Ed, they had no commando knives.

5.53 Ed Maltby (former Spaldington Patrol) with the SAS in Norway, 1945. (Ed Maltby)

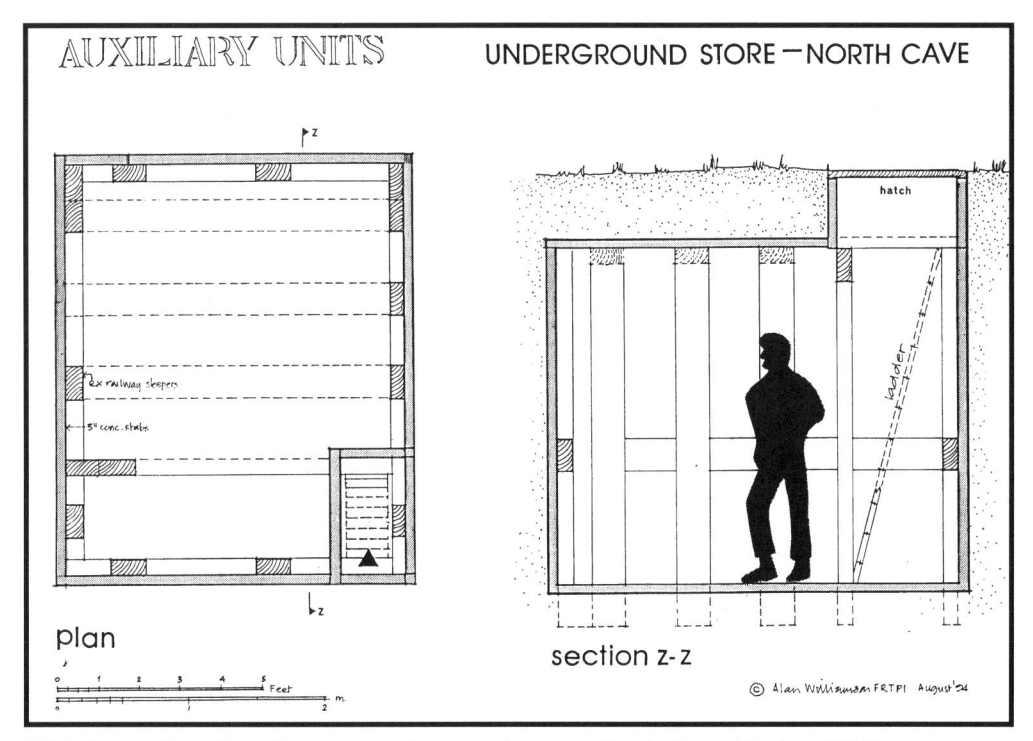

5.54 Survey Drawing of mystery underground store at North Cave. (Author 1994)

5.55 Charlie Mason at the partially destroyed store at North Cave. (Author)

5.56 Charlie Mason measuring the remains of a bunk bed believed to be from the North Cave underground store. (Author 1994)

5.4 The Mystery Bunker

About 600 yards (550m) to the south-west of the North Cave OB is a mysterious deep hole in the middle of a wood. Somewhat sinister in appearance it is the remains of a wartime underground structure. The roof has almost entirely collapsed, allowing both rain and surface water to fill the bottom 2-3ft (0.6-0.9m). The only surface remains are the entrance shaft and adjoining, unstable roof section. The remains of the original wooden ladder protrude from the water's surface.

The whole structure measures 10' 3" (3.1m) long x 8' 6" (2.6m) wide. Probing, at depth, has revealed a possible floor level of about 10ft (3m) below ground level. The original internal height, covered by 2ft (0.6m) of overburden, was 7' 10" (2.35m).

The internal walls were riveted with vertical concrete slabs, 42" x 21" x 3" (10.1m x 0.5m x 76mm) held in place by a bracing of wooden railway sleepers. The roof may have been of similar construction, making the whole bunker exceedingly strong, much greater than that required for the standard OB.

There is no evidence of any ventilation or other features normally associated with living conditions. There is no escape hatch or tunnel. It has all the appearance of a secret, underground store, possibly for ammunition and explosives. However, nearby, are the remains of a single 'bunk bed' wooden frame covered with a wire mesh. One unusual feature is the existence of two ring bolts screwed into one end of the frame, giving the impression that this had been a fold away bed, possibly used for emergencies.

The overall size of this bed fits neatly into a space in the bunker created by the entrance shaft. The use of such a bed may have been required if exit had been prevented due to the presence of nearby enemy forces.

Many former Auxiliary Unit members, both East Riding and elsewhere, have been asked their views on this particular store. None has been aware of its existence or of similar examples. It is obviously professionally built, most likely by a military construction team. Similar structures appear in various pre-war military field-engineering manuals.

What is known, that in early 1940, various government agencies were covertly burying stockpiles of ammunition and explosives for possible use in the event of an invasion. Additionally Col. Gubbins, in his first report (July 1940) on the setting up of the Auxiliary Units, refers to both 'dumps' and "to distribute and conceal the special stores." These references are in addition to the stocking of hide-outs (OBs).

The military or Home Guard did not generally hide their ammunition, especially in such remote situations. The best possible view of its use is as a central, secret, ammunition/explosive store from which to re-supply the nearest Auxiliary Unit Groups. Knowledge of its existence would have been severely restricted to the IO and possibly senior group leaders. It makes much sense, not to have such a facility close to the invasion coast, where it could have been most certainly overrun.

However, the mystery remains. Hopefully publication of its existence may produce the correct answer in time.

6. Special Duties Branch

6.1 Background

One of the most important factors in any conflict, is the precise knowledge of your enemy's location, strength and activities. This intelligence needs to be gathered quickly and discreetly.

To assist the regular forces in this role, a second branch was formed within the Auxiliary Units, known as Special Duties. This arm of the 'cloak and dagger' unit was obviously more cloak than dagger, so much so that in the early days HQ staff had difficulty in locating their own field operatives.

Originally, it was thought that this Special Duty Branch was formed somewhat later than the Operational Branch, possibly in 1942. However, the discovery of secret reports in the Public Record Office suggests that Intelligence was an original part of 1940 setup. There was, however, a major expansion of the network in 1941/42, and this may have contributed to the earlier presumptions.

To maintain the secrecy element of the overall project, neither Branch, except at HQ level, was informed of the other's existence.

The Special Duties Intelligence network consisted of a chain of radio stations manned by either regular forces or civilians, feeding information into Army HQs. This information would have initially been collected by a small army of strategically located civilian 'spies'. The records reveal that a total of 3250 civilians were secretly involved in the Special Duties branch. They were mainly recruited by Intelligence Officers of the Special Duties branch, who were each responsible for one of ten areas within the likely invasion coastal belt.

Unlike the saboteurs of the Operational Branch this new group of civilians consisted of both men and women, age and physical fitness not being of paramount importance. They were not issued with weapons or military clothing, their normal civilian clothing being the perfect cover for this role. However, training was given in the preparation of simple intelligence reports, and how to carry out their duties without attracting undue attention.

In a select number of cases, those chosen to be radio operators, were given additional instruction in the use of the newly designed, voice transmission, short wave radio sets.

Most of these volunteers would be in reserved categories or exempt military service. In their normal day to day occupations, such as postmen, farm workers, milk roundsmen, doctors and health visitors, they would be able to move around towns, villages and the countryside behind enemy lines without undue suspicion.

6.2 The Intelligence Network

Control Stations (In-Stas)
Strategically placed around the invasion coastal areas were a series of secret radio stations manned by either Royal Signals or ATS personnel. The exact number of stations is as yet unknown, but possibly 20+, and generally located in or near a Divisional Army HQ, which would in the

6.1 A garden shed provided secret access to the underground radio station at Goathland Out-Stas. The nearby tree, with 'early warning' bird box, carries the co-axial radio wires embedded in the trunk. (Author 1995)

6.2 The trap door in the garden shed floor reveals the entrance to the underground radio station at Goathland Out-Stas. (Author 1995)

6.3 The wooden ventilation ducts in Goathland Out-Stas. (Author 1995)

event of an invasion assume direct control. These stations were known as control or In Stas. Each would control and maintain a group of 5-10 civilian radio stations known as 'Out Stas'

The standard Control Station would consist of two separate elements, a hut or building on the surface and a nearby secret underground base. The latter would only be used in the actual event of an invasion, at which time the surface element would be abandoned.

Both parts of the Control Station would contain a high frequency, short wave, radio set designed and built by the Special Duties Section of the Royal Signals. They were used for transmitting and receiving voice coded messages operating on the pre-war BBC Television wavebands (60-65 megacycles). The use of supposedly redundant wavebands proved a successful part of the cover, and appears to have gone un-noticed by the German authorities. The radio sets themselves were extremely small, being contained within a wood or strong cardboard carrying case measuring only 18" x 12" x 6" (46cm x 30cm x 15cm). They were powered by a heavy duty 6 volt battery. Forty foot (12m) copper aerials were strung amongst the high branches of nearby trees or secretly disguised on buildings i.e. behind lightning conductors. This was a dangerous task, as the Royal Signals personnel almost became trapeze artists amongst the trees, with at least one receiving fatal injuries. When trees were used, the radio down leads would be cut into the tree trunk and hidden behind the bark or a coloured cement infill.

Those stations, manned by Royal Signals personnel would consist of two radio operators and one instrument mechanic. Others were manned by ATS Officers, specially recruited for the clarity of their voices, who were often affectionately referred to as the 'secret sweeties'. Their role was to monitor the radio messages from the civilian Out-Stas, and pass the information onto the Special Duties HQ at Hannington Hall near Coleshill Auxiliary Units HQ in Wiltshire. In some cases the information would initially be sent to an Area HQ positioned further inland. The Royal Signals personnel would also have to visit all the civilian Out-Stas to supply recharged batteries and check the aerials etc.

The underground Control stations consisted of 2 or 3 separate chambers, with a vertical ladder entrance at one end and a horizontal escape tunnel at the opposite end. They were, in many instances, similar to the underground bases of the Operational Branch in that entrances and exits were disguised by cantilevered tree trunks and other sliding mechanisms. They contained bunk beds, tables/desks, food, water and a petrol generator for charging the radio batteries. They became known as Zero Stations as their station number had a zero prefix.

In addition to their normal duties, the Control Stations played an important role by monitoring radio transmissions for possible German agents, and even breaches in our own security network. This monitoring became particularly essential during the Allied preparations for Operation Overlord (D-Day) and the complex decoy planning.

Out Stations (Out Stas)

The civilian operated stations had no standard design or location. They could be in sheds, follies (such as the mausoleum at Brocklesby Park in Lincolnshire), underground dugouts, cellars or warehouses. One underground station near Goathland, North Yorkshire, was entered via trapdoor in the floor of a small garden shed. Some later examples constructed by special Royal Engineer Companies followed a similar pattern to those of the Zero station, Goathland again being a classic

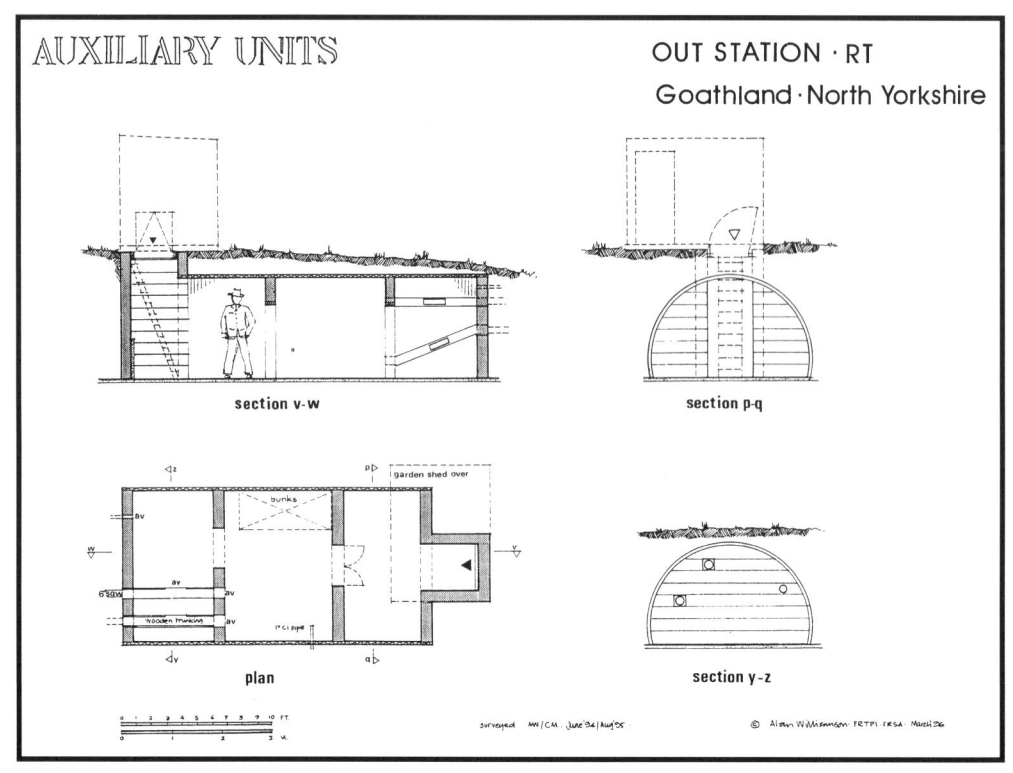

6.4 Survey drawing of Goathland Out-stas. (Author 1995)

6.5 Hannington Hall, Wiltshire, wartime accommodation for the Special Duties Branch of the Auxiliary Units. (Author 2001)

example. Their precise number is still uncertain possibly 150+, with about 55 being known along the east coast of England and Scotland.

They appeared to have been manned by two civilian volunteers, who would obviously work in shift pattern to prevent the entire network being bought to a sudden stop should one become, for various reasons, unavailable.

Intelligence Report/Spies

Information on the enemy would be delivered, sometimes indirectly, to the out-stations by a small army of intelligence gatherers or 'spies'. To maintain the secrecy of both the identity of their counterpart radio operators and actual location, messages for transmission would be left in secret 'letterboxes' near out-stations for later collection. In some cases, messages would be moved from 'letter box' to 'letter box' by other personnel known as 'cut-outs'. These letter boxes could be any agreed location, such as a particular drainpipe or culvert, a hollow tree trunk or even behind a telegraph pole number plate. In at least one case messages were delivered to an underground radio station by rolling a split tennis ball, containing a message, direct into a ventilation pipe.

6.6 Lieut Kirk Chapel RE (later Captain), at his wedding in September 1944 at Hornsea, to Joy Hollis, sister of Capt Peter Hollis. (Mrs Anne Hollis)

6.3 East Riding – Special Duties Branch

Research into this branch of the Auxiliary Units, its personnel and network, has been the most difficult. Any Public Record Office information, on the various radio stations and people involved, has yet to surface. The problem has been compounded by the reluctance of the few known surviving members of the civilian network to discuss their wartime operations.

However, subsequent investigation and chance finds have revealed parts of the East Riding network, but as yet no substantiated information has been found regarding the 'spy' element of the branch. This may be due to the fact that during their active service period many were already early to middle age and have long been deceased, their oath of strict secrecy being kept to the grave.

Fortunately David Lampe's book, 'The Last Ditch', revealed the location of the East Riding Zero Station as being at South Dalton. Since then civilian out-stations have been discovered at Rudston and Sigglesthorne.

David Lampe also suggested that there had been a Control (Zero) Station at Garrowby Hall, which was owned by Lord Halifax.

This appears to have been confused with Hickleton Hall, near Doncaster, also owned by Lord Halifax. In fact Miss Beatrice Temple, the former Senior Commander in charge of the Special Duty ATS operators, was reported in a press interview in 1968, as stating that there were only two control stations in Yorkshire, namely at South Dalton and Hickleton Hall. She was billeted at Hickleton Hall for four months from October 1942. Her former Junior Commander, Barbara Culleton, has more recently recalled being billeted in the summer house (gazebo?) at Hickleton Hall in September 1941.

There is, however, an unsubstantiated local tale, that during the war, a radio set was hidden behind a pile of wood at Garrowby Hall. If true, this may have been another Out-Stas.

According to Arthur Gabbitas, both South Dalton and Canwick Hall (Lincoln) Control Stations relayed messages to Hickleton Hall, which was the Area HQ.

South Dalton Control Station

Initial assistance in locating the precise area for the Control Station, near South Dalton, was helpfully given by Mr D Hutchinson, who had farmed nearby, and been the local Home Guard commander. Apparently, he was shown the concealed entrance shaft at the end of the War, but had wisely declined to descend into what was, and is still now, a dark, hazardous, underground labyrinth.

In more recent years, it was rumoured locally that the underground radio station had been demolished by a Royal Engineers Unit, and the resulting cavity backfilled. A preliminary site investigation to check this story revealed an area of loosely packed disturbed soil containing fragments of corrugated metal sheeting and piping. In fact, all the elements suggesting the existence of a destroyed underground structure. However, there was no evidence of any brick or blockwork debris, and the investigation continued into the surrounding area. A chance probing, at depth, revealed evidence of a curved steel roof some 2 ½ ft (0.58m) below ground level.

6.7 Search for remains of underground South Dalton Control Station, allegedly destroyed at the end of World War II. (Author 1998)

6.8 Drilling through the reinforced concrete entrance cap of the South Dalton Control Station. (Author's coll.)

6.9 Entrance shaft exposed at the South Dalton Control Station. (Author's coll.)

Further mechanical excavation exposed the hidden entrance shaft that had been sealed with an in-situ concrete capping. The use of military, barbed wire, picket posts as reinforcing rods suggests that this work may have been done at the end of the war.

The original top of the 3ft square (0.9m) entrance shaft had been deliberately lowered to hide its presence. This had been achieved by removal of the top layer of concrete blocks, and re-covering with 12" (305mm) of soil. The shaft descended to a depth of 9'.6" (2.9m) with any ladder or steps having long since been removed.

The anticipation of entering this underground chamber, sealed for about 53 years, had almost the same excitement as Howard Carter's 1923 archaeological excavation of King Tutenkhamen's burial chamber in Egypt.

In a similar manner, this underground radio station was still structurally intact, and also contained 'grave goods'. The latter were not made of precious metals, jewels or carvings, but just as important, being the remains of the fittings and furniture required in its operational days.

This proved to be the most complete Zero Station yet discovered, and therefore of national importance. It comprises a Nissen hut type structure buried underground with access via the previously described concrete shaft. This half round hut is made of heavy gauge corrugated steel standing on a floor of precast concrete slabs. Like the entrance hatch, all end and internal wall divisions are constructed using 9" (230mm) hollow concrete blocks.

The total length, from the entrance hatch to the start of the escape tunnel at the opposite end, is 25'.6" (7.8m). The width, at the widest point, is 10'.2" (3.2m) with a maximum height of 6'.7" (2.3m) The length is subdivided into three unequal chambers, with the main centre one accessed by 4'.9" (1.4m) doorways.

The first chamber, leading from the entrance shaft, measured 10'.2" x 5'.0" (3.3m x 1.5m) and contained a 42 gallon (191 litre) galvanised water tank mounted on supporting brickwork. Water into this was fed via a cast iron pipe emerging, externally, near ground level. Two, salt-glazed pipes acted as ventilation shafts bringing fresh air from ground level. One of these pipes also acted as a conduit for the water feed pipe.

The principal features were two adjoining wooden shelf units, containing some rusty tins and bottles, which both swivelled outwards to reveal a hidden door leading to the main chamber. This wooden door appeared to have an inner core of loose sand, possibly for soundproofing, should the enemy have gained entry to access chamber. It may even have provided a bullet resistant barrier.

The main or inner chamber, measuring 11'.0" x 10'.2" (3.3m x 3.2m), was where the operators would have lived and worked. It contained some painted wooden furniture, and a mass of wiring/shelving etc which had been ripped off the walls.

The furniture consisted of a desk, with a writing slope, 3'.0" x 2'.6" x 2'.6" high (914mm x 762mm x 762mmn), and a table, 3'.0" x 2'.2" x 2'.6" (914mm x 660mm x 762mm) covered with a thin metal sheet. It would appear that the beds had been removed prior to the sealing operation.

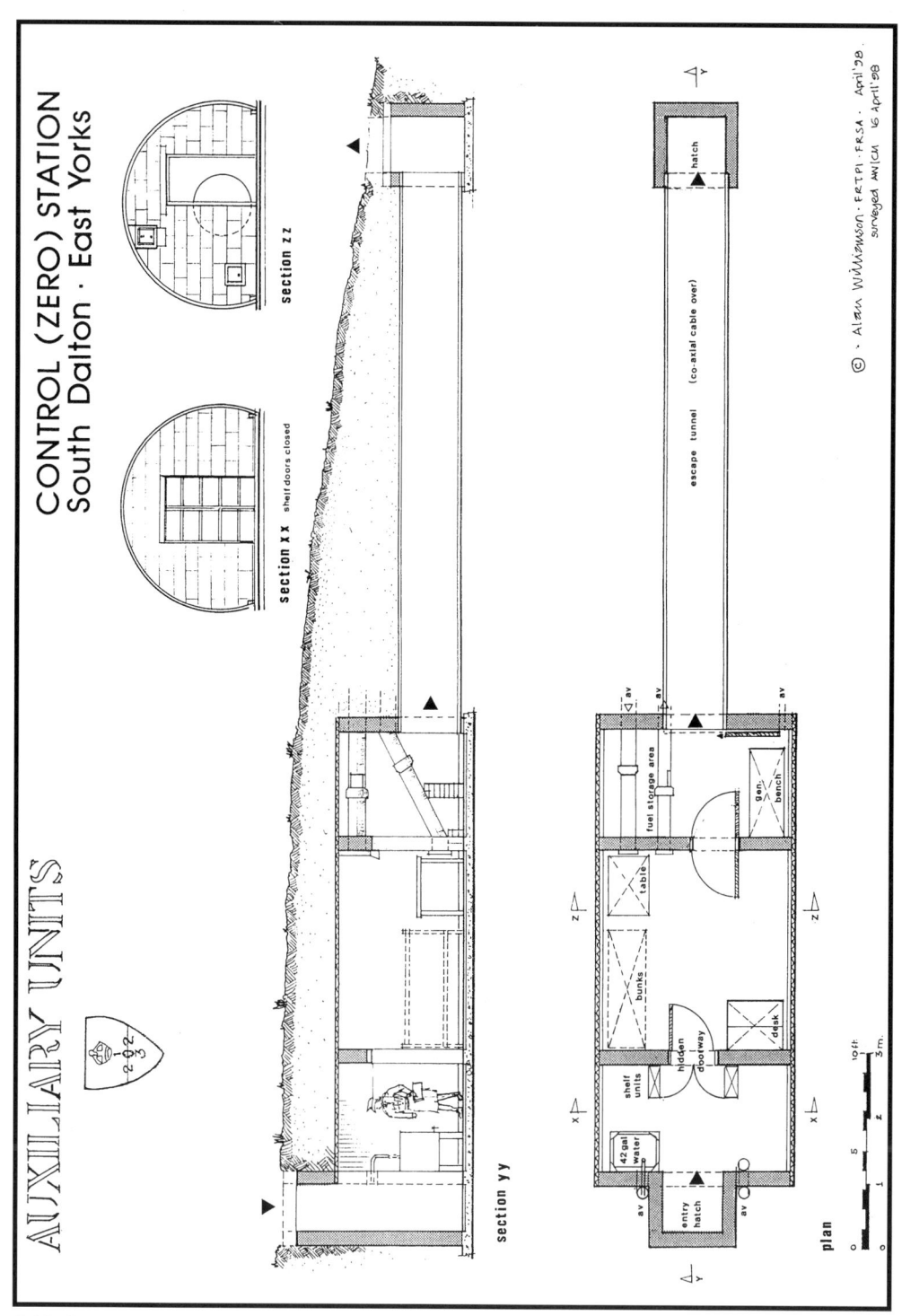

6.10 Survey Drawing of South Dalton Control (Zero) Station. (Author 1998)

6.11 Interior view of South Dalton Control (Zero) Station, showing collapsed generator bench and improvised fire bucket. (Author 1998)

6.12 Interior view of South Dalton Control (Zero) Station showing operator's wooden desk, and part of original trapdoor discarded when the entrance was sealed. (Author 1998)

6.13 One of the pair of shelf units which swing out to reveal the secret doorway to the South Dalton Control (Zero) Station inner radio chamber. (Author 1998)

Amongst the mass of wiring was a brass 9 volt bulb holder attached to fabric covered flex. There also were four lengths of aerial co-axial cable, varying from 15ft to 19½ft (4.6m to 5.9m) Also lying on the floor, were two metal pipes 3ft (0.9m) in length, which revolved in wooden end brackets, rather like the traditional towel roller. Fastenings on the corrugated side wall indicated where they had been fixed, one above the other but at some distance apart. Their possible use was for maps or charts which would have wound between the two rollers.

Another interesting find was part of the entrance shaft wooden hatch, to which a curved tree branch had been fastened down with hessian tape to form a lifting handle. Coupled with other natural debris on the woodland floor this handle formed part of a most ingenious disguise.

The two ventilation shafts in this inner mini chamber still retained their fittings, including the metal remains of a patent, mechanical, extraction device which may have been power operated.

A further doorway led to the third and final chamber. This contained a wooden bench 4'.6" x 2'.0" x 1'.11" high (1377mm x 609mm x 584mm), the top of which had wooden mounting blocks for a small petrol generator. This would have been used for charging batteries, for both the radio and ancillary lighting. Under this bench was a fire bucket, made out of a large rectangular metal food container, with a simple wooden handle bridging the open top.

On opposite walls were the painted words, petrol (red paint) and paraffin (blue paint) to indicate where the appropriate fuel cans should be stored, a very necessary safety factor in a semi-darkened working environment.

On the opposite side to the generator bench were two 10" diameter (254mm) concrete asbestos ventilation pipes leading from the outside into the main chamber. At the end wall, a sliding wooden hatch, 3'.4" x 3'.0" (1016mm x 914mm), concealed an escape tunnel 31ft (9.4m) in length. This was made out 3'.0" diam (914mm) precast concrete drainage pipes with an exit shaft, 3'.6" square (1066mm) constructed of hollow concrete blocks. In a similar manner to the entrance shaft, the top had been lowered and sealed with a concrete capping.

There was no evidence of the external radio aerial, the mature trees which would have contained it have long since been felled.

About 300yards (274m) away lie the remains of the, above ground, Control Station partially hidden by woodland. It consisted of a Nissen hut type structure measuring 19ftx17ft (5.79mx5.18m) with brick ends wall and entrance porch. The porch also contains a separate cubicle for a chemical toilet. All that remains today is one end brick wall and the entrance porch. The corrugated steel roof has long since been removed, and the other wall and internal partition have collapsed.

However, a nearby mature beech tree still contains the co-axial wireless cable, which protrudes from the bark at the upper levels.

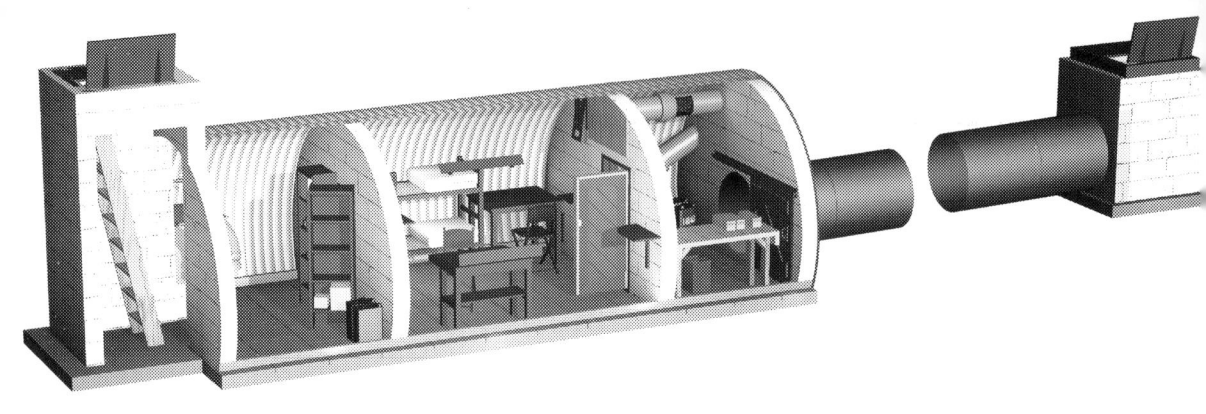

6.14 Reconstruction drawing of South Dalton Control (Zero) Station. (Simon Williamson. Copyright)

6.15 Reconstruction drawing of South Dalton Control (Zero) Station rear generator chambers and escape tunnel. (Simon Williamson. Copyright)

6.16 Reconstruction drawing of South Dalton Control (Zero) Station inner radio chamber. (Simon Williamson.Copyright)

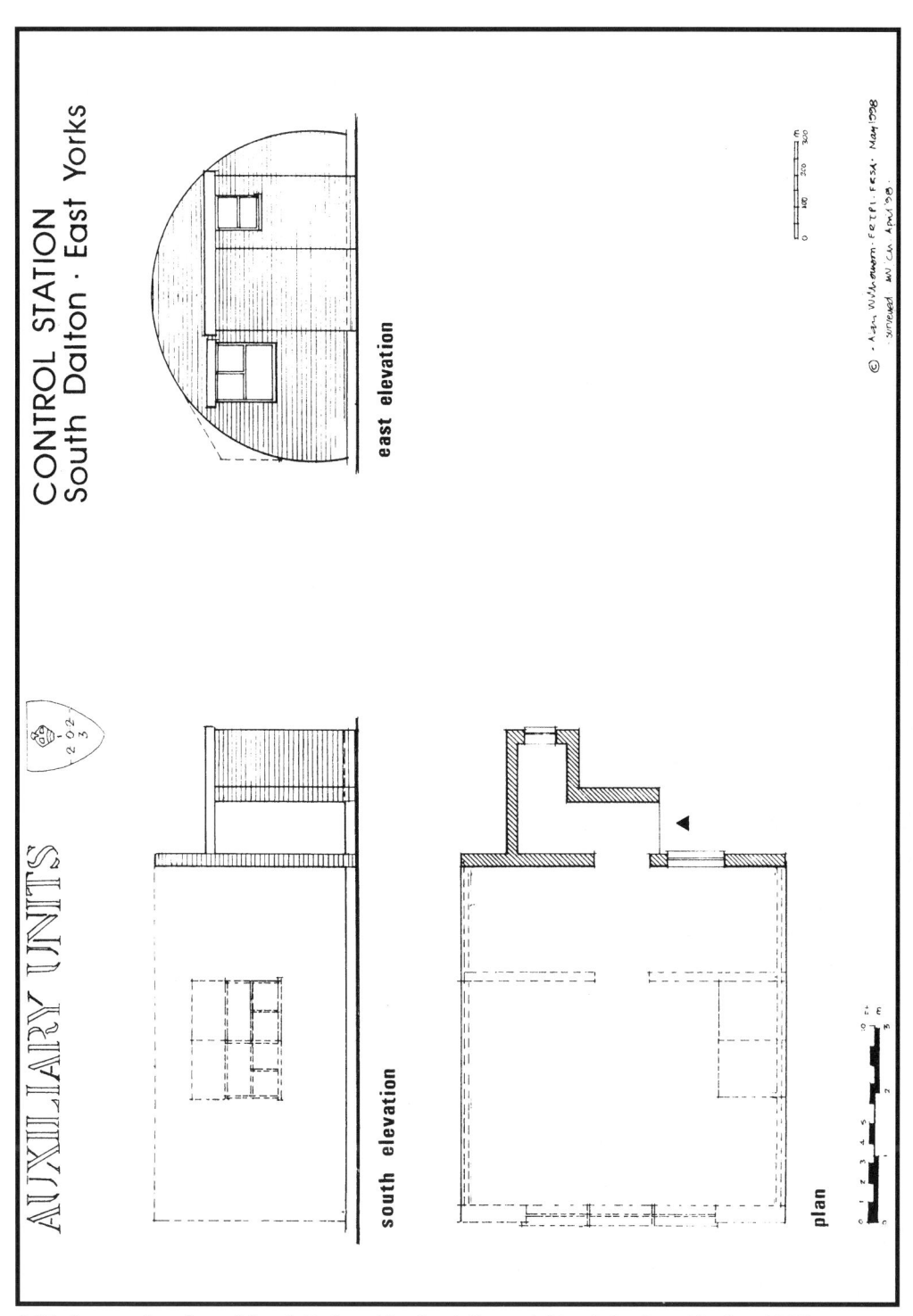

6.17 Survey drawing of South Dalton 'Surface' Control (Zero) Station. (Author 1998)

Rudston Out-Stas

This lies on the south facing slope of the Gypsey Race valley near the village of Rudston. The actual site is built into the side of a small chalk pit surrounded by mature woodland.

Possibly the first members of the public to discover this was a Bridlington Scout troop, which was camping in the area at the end of the Second World War. Being in a clearing, the site of the underground bunker was an ideal place to light a camp fire - but not on top of the wooden entrance hatch!

Bernard Langton, one of the original Bridlington Scouts, recalls entering the bunker via a ladder and finding a table and telephone in the inner chamber. There may have been other features, but the cursory inspection was 57 years ago and in a chamber without any lighting.

In size and layout, it is almost identical to the Control Station at South Dalton. The major differences are that it is built much closer to the ground surface and has a shorter escape tunnel, 12ft (3.65m) which exits into the steep side of the old chalk pit.

Today all internal fittings, other than one broken wooden inner door, have disappeared. Unlike the South Dalton Control Station, the internal ventilation system had been made out of square wooden trunking instead of drainage pipes. The Out-Stas, near Goathland, still retains the original wooden trunking, and appears to be the only such surviving example. The entrance hatch has been sealed with a concrete capping, the only access now being via the escape tunnel, foxes and other wildlife permitting.

A nearby tree still contains the down lead of the co-axial wireless cable, with ample evidence of the aerial cable, originally strung between trees, lying broken in small lengths on the woodland floor. It is understood that the two civilian operators were Bill Gatenby and Dr Leonard Watson, a GP from Bridlington. Both have now passed away.

6.18 Remains of South Dalton 'Surface' Control (Zero) Station. The nissen hut structure has collapsed with only one end brick wall and the entrance lobby remaining (Author 1998)

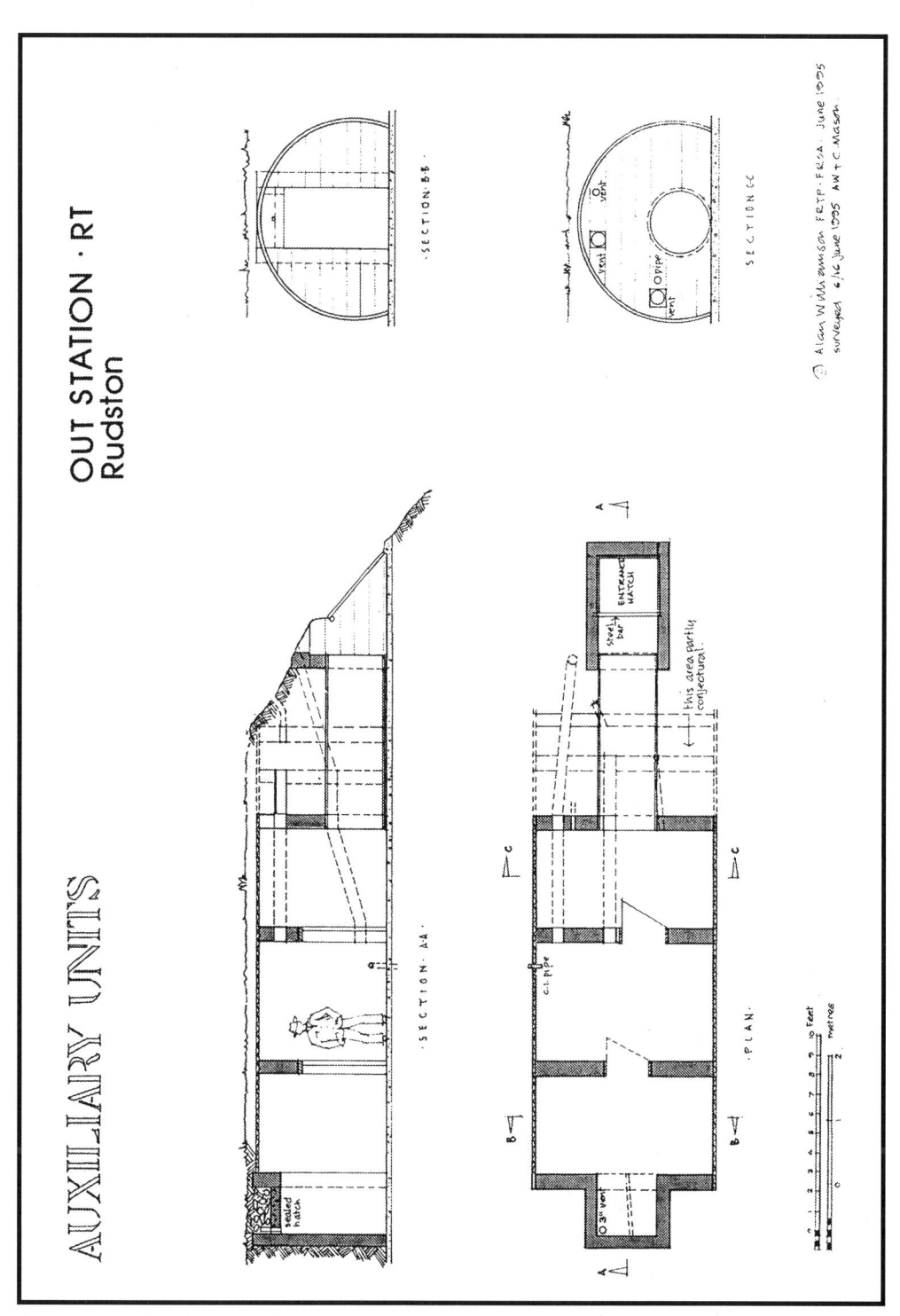

6.19 Survey drawing of Rudston Out Station. (Author 1995)

6.20 Rudston Out Station, showing tunnel exit into quarry side. (Author 1998)

6.21 Charlie Mason 'escaping' from Rudston Out Station via tunnel exit. (Author 1998)

6.22 Charlie Mason in Rudston Out Station inner chamber looking towards the escape tunnel entrance. (Author 1998)

Sigglesthorne Out-Stas

This underground civilian radio station was discovered and recorded by George Dawes and Mark Bond, two fellow researchers with the Defence of Britain Project.

It was concealed within a shelter belt wood on the edge of Sigglesthorne village, and had apparently been sealed since the end of World War II. Two nearby trees had grooves cut into the bark extending for about 30ft (9m). One still contained the co-axial aerial cable embedded in the bark.

This underground bunker comprised two, unequal sized chambers, with walls constructed from 9" (230mm) concrete blocks. The overall size was 10ft (3.0m) wide x 13'10" (4.252m) long x 7' (2.1m) high, with a concrete floor. The roof consisted of two 1/8" (3mm) steel plates bolted together with a central angle iron support. Over this was laid a 8" (200mm) concrete slab.

The first chamber contained the entrance hatch in the roof, from down which access was gained via eight metal rungs fixed to the wall. This ante chamber, measuring 6' (1.8m) x 4'7" (1.40m) contained a bilge pump and floor sump, both obviously very essential items considering that the chamber, when first opened, was submerged in 3'8" (1.1m) of water. This required pumping out prior to access. A 4" s.g.w pipe, near roof level, acted as the ventilation outlet.

In a like manner to other underground radio stations, the entrance doorway into the main chamber was concealed behind a wooden shelf unit, which swung aside on hinges. Behind this was the remains of the standard blackout material hung across the doorway. This main chamber measuring 6'1" (1.85m) wide x 6'9" (2.06m), contained a wooden bench/desk and a wooden table, similar to those found at the main Control Station (Zero Station) at South Dalton. There was also an Elsan chemical toilet, behind which there was a 4" s.g.w ventilation inlet pipe. Within the main chamber there were four further ventilation pipes, two inlet near the floor and two outlet near the roof.

There were also two steel pipes entering from the roof area, one containing the ends of four co-axial radio cables, and the other possibly being the filler inlet pipe for a water storage tank.

The local story is that its construction was disguised by the nearby temporary siting of a Bofors anti-aircraft gun, which would have presented reasonable explanation for such military activity in this woodland. Similar ruses were much used elsewhere.

Mrs Joy Chapel recalls that her late husband, Captain Kirk Chapel, pointed this, and other sites, out to her during a visit after the war. In 1941/42, as a Lieutenant in charge of a special Royal Engineer detachment, he was responsible for the construction of many Auxiliary Unit bunkers stretching from Alnwick, Northumberland to the Lincolnshire coast. During his time in the East Riding, his detachment was based in a requisitioned house opposite the Floral Hall in Hornsea. Mrs Joy Chapel was the sister of Captain Peter Hollis, the Intelligence Officer of the East Riding Auxiliary Units. This proved that secrets are best kept within the family!

It is understood that the two civilian operators were Christian Smith, the landowner and a Peter Dunne.

6.23 Sigglesthorne Out Station entrance shaft showing steps using steel 'dog spikes'. The hand operated bilge pump can be seen bottom centre. (George Dawes 1998)

6.25 Sigglesthorne Out Station – Elsan chemical toilet still in-situ. (George Dawes 1998)

6.24 Sigglesthorne Out Station – wooden desk and table showing effect of years of immersion in ground water. (George Dawes, 1998)

Other Out-Stas

The only other confirmed Out-Stas relates to a warehouse in Hull. Stan Judd, a former Royal Signals Corporal attached to the Auxiliary Units Special Duties Section at Canwick Hall Lincoln, has recalled visiting a warehouse in Hull, where the radio set was concealed behind a pile of sacks on the top floor. Unfortunately he could not remember the name or actual location of the premises. Apparently, Stan Judd made regular trips over the Humber bringing fresh batteries for the various Out-Stas radios. He also checked the radio aerials strung amongst the trees. He remembered meeting a "Home Guard Officer" in High Street Bridlington who was associated with an Out-Stas built in the side of a quarry (possibly Rudston?)

Spurn was another suggested location for an Out-Stas but was rejected due to reception difficulties. If there was an alternative site in this Holderness area it has yet to be found. However a recent report has suggested that a local farmer kept a secret radio in a locked room in his farmhouse at Out Newton. This would have been an ideal location, situated on high ground overlooking the North Sea. Also in the Holderness area, there has been a recent report that a Paull village shopkeeper had been selected for covert 'eyes and ears' operations during the War. This may possibly have been part of the Special Duties Branch. Both at Boynton and Sewerby there is evidence of underground wartime structures which have no connection with the local Auxiliary Unit patrols. Further investigation may establish a link with the radio network.

Finally, there were reports of a radio operator in the grounds of Hymers College in Hull. Apparently, aerial cables were found hung in a tree, with the suspicion that a German spy was operating in the area, and detecting apparatus was placed at an upper room in the college. A recent inspection of the College grounds, whilst an obvious place for an Out-Stas, found no physical evidence of any such operation.

6.26 Drawing of Sigglesthorne Out Station based on original survey by George Dawes. (Author 2003)

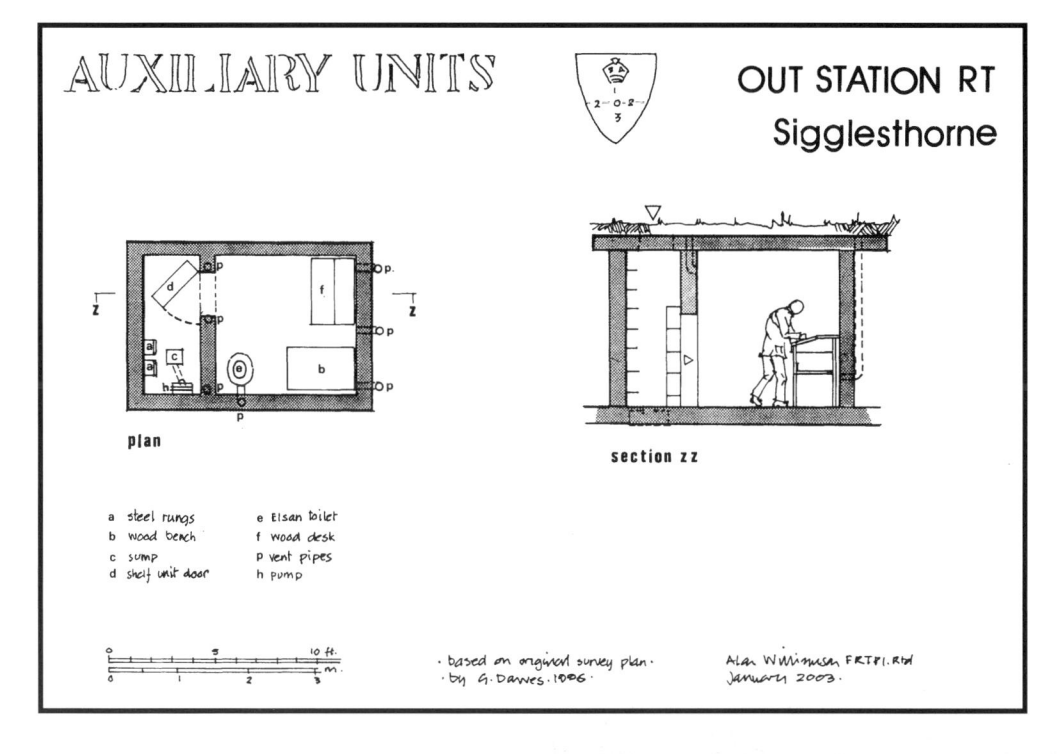

7. THE STAND DOWN

In 1943, with the tide of war gradually turning in favour of the Allies, preparations were in hand for the D-Day landings in occupied France. The UK was becoming a vast arsenal of weaponry and invasion equipment. However, whilst it was also teeming with millions of Allied servicemen going through their intensive training, more manpower was continually being sought for the build-up.

Any military personnel, that could be spared, were being re-drafted for the D-Day Force. The threat of a German invasion was gradually receding and the official view was still *"that invasion was still possible but improbable. This being the case, it is now unnecessary to retain a force for operations under invasion conditions alone."*

There was, therefore, a sudden flurry of paper relating to the heading of "Economy in Manpower". Serious suggestions were coming down from Whitehall re the closing down of the Auxiliary Units, which were essentially an anti-invasion organisation requiring administration by scarce regular forces personnel.

These views were naturally being severely contested by those with more intimate knowledge of the value of the Auxiliary Units. In fact, their own Commander in his briefing note dealing with the 'Reduction or Withdrawal of Regular Personnel' wrote that:

"Although not in my province to decide or in any way influence, I wish to state emphatically that there is no possibility of running the Operation Branch entirely under H G (Home Guard) auspices. For nearly four years Auxiliaries, who were hand picked men, have had rubbed unto them that they are part of the regular army and G H Q troops and as such were expected to give at least two or three times the amount of time training that the HG did. This they have willingly and selflessly done and achieved an esprit-de-corps second to none. They regard themselves, quite properly, as a corps d'elite and something superior to any Home Guard. They have had repeated assurances that they would never be asked to revert to Home Guard. You might just as well expect a Guards regiment to amalgamate with the Salvation Army. It isn't on! They must either continue to tick over with a greatly reduced regular cadre or be told they can "stand-down". Whether it is acceptable for the pick of the Home Guard to stand-down before the rest is a question of high policy with many tricky aspects."

However, he concluded his report with a recommendation that the Operational Branch should continue under a skeleton staff until the HQ stand-down, and close down all the Special Duty Branch except certain specific vulnerable areas.

A similar view was forcibly made by Lt. General Franklin, Commander in Chief GHQ Home Forces, in a letter dated 6 September 1943 to the Under-Secretary of State, the War Office, stating that:

"1. Auxiliary Units are an extremely valuable organisation in invasion conditions. Once disbanded they cannot be reformed and invasion has not yet been ruled out for the rest of the war.
2. In the event of a raid, the Operational Sections form lightning patrols to cut off the withdrawal of the enemy, while Special Duties sections are a valuable alternative means of obtaining information concerning movements of the raiding forces

3. If disbanded, the Home Guard in the Operational Sections would return to their original battalions and would spread the impression that, as they are no longer required, there would be no need for the Home Guard as a whole. Further, there would be a grave danger of a breach of security regarding the work which Auxiliary Units have been carrying out.

……..7. Finally, I consider that the value to be obtained in other forms of service from the regular personnel would be quite incommensurate with the breaking up of this Unit to which I attach great importance. It would also be a poor tribute to the magnificent body of Home Guard and civilians who have given untiring and unceasing work to their country for three years. As stated, however, a reduction in establishment of 8 officer and 50 other ranks can now be made with possibly further small savings, while 12 officers who are category 'A' could be exchanged with category 'B' if suitable officers can be found."

7.1   Group of senior NCOs at Station 1090, Weathersfield SAS Re-supply Dept. Sgt Harry Nicholson (former Cottingham South Patrol) is 1st left, rear row. (Mrs Susan Pace coll.)

1943/44 saw a gradual reduction in the regular personnel at Auxiliary Units HQ at Coleshill until only a small cadre remained. One of the major 'casualties' of the reduction were the Scout Patrols, whose training role was now virtually handed over to the local Patrol Group leaders.

Many of the actual Auxiliary Unit patrol members were being recalled to the regular forces. This presented somewhat of a security risk should their previous role be revealed. They were therefore quickly identified and generally placed in units with other Auxiliary Unit members. Their training and background made them ideal candidates for recruitment to the various commando units. Lord Lovat, in particular sought them out for his famous Lovat Scouts, and others volunteered for SAS.

The decision to retain the Operational Branch proved later to be a wise decision. At the time of immediate preparations for the D-Day landings, there was a real danger, should the invasion not be entirely successful, that Hitler could launch raiding parties in an attempt to seize the Isle of Wight. This could have seriously threatened the Allies major re-supply base at Portsmouth. Therefore to guard the island Auxiliary Unit patrol members, from areas outside the south coast, were asked to volunteer for this duty. Many did volunteer, including East Riding members, the cover story being that they were to guard German prisoners being brought back from the invasion beach-heads.

By July 1944, with the Allied invasion going well, the War Office decided that they could now dispense with the Special Duties Branch, thus releasing more regular personnel for active service. By letter dated 4th July 1944, General Franklin, Commander in Chief GHQ Home Forces, informed the Commander, Auxiliary Units to this effect. In the letter he praised the work they had done and requested that a copy of *"this letter be sent to all members of the Special Duties organisation as my own acknowledgement of the value and efficiency of their work."*

With regard to the Operational Branch, administration was handed over to the three Territorial Army Association (TAA) located at Inverness, York and Reading. The York TAA was based at 9 St Leonard's, York, and looked after the 202 Battalion, GHQ Res, which comprised all Auxiliary Units from North Yorkshire to the Thames. The East Riding formed part of 202 Battalion. Furthermore to reduce the number of regular personnel the former 20 separate areas were now amalgamated into four regions:-

No 1 Region	-	Scottish Command
No 2 Region	-	Northern Command
No 3 Region	-	Eastern and South Eastern Commands
No 4 Region	-	Southern and Western Commands

No 2 Region, covering the east coast from Northumberland to the Thames, had its HQ located in Beverley at No 33 North Bar Within. This chance discovery came about from an address on the bottom of a report dealing with some Auxiliary Units administration in Lincolnshire.

Further research has revealed the HQ was secretly located at the rear of, and over, a sweet and tobacconist's shop. The original door from the shop into the rear quarters had been sealed up, and a new entrance made into the side street. None of the surviving local members appear to have been aware of its existence. It almost mirrors the Highworth Post Office, which doubled as the secret front for the nearby Auxiliary Units HQ at Coleshill.

With the reduction in the number of areas, and regular personnel, the need for Intelligence Officers had been halved. Only the less fit had been retained. However, to assist with local control, selected Auxiliary Units Group Patrol leaders were promoted to act as Area Group Patrol Commanders. The former East Riding area was now split into two sub areas, with an Area Group Commander in charge of each. They had the back-up of an Assistant Area Group Commander and Group Clerks.

One of the last important acts of the Auxiliary Units was to afford extra protection for the King and Queen. In July 1944, with the war going against Hitler, there was a serious suggestion that an attempt could be made, by possibly a paratroop raiding force, to capture the King and hold him hostage. The most likely place for this to occur was Balmoral Castle, which was less heavily defended than either Buckingham Palace or Windsor Castle.

In a top secret letter, dated 21 July 1944, a request was made for Col. Douglas (Commander, Auxiliary Units) to meet General Thorne (GOC Scottish Command) at Balmoral Castle on the 29th July to discuss the question of Auxiliary Units taking part in the defence of the Castle. A manuscript note on this letter dated 21 July, reads:

"The situation is as follows:
I suggest to Col. Douglas that he might help by finding auxiliaries to guard at Balmoral, because the 5 Manchester (the regular battalion provided) are weak………. Tell Col.Douglas to meet Gen. Thorne as arranged to discuss the plan which MGGS and Col. Douglas talked about……"

In March 1995, the Sunday Express published an article under the heading "Did Nazis Have a Secret Plot to Seize the Royal Family." According to the newspaper, Major Wilf Bramble, Auxiliary Unit HQ communications officer, was ordered to build hides (OBs) at Balmoral Castle. Two hides were built, the larger one to house up to 12 men, and the smaller one for back up purposes. They were linked by radio to the Castle and the Garrison. The story was that in the event of a German raid, the King and Queen would be rushed away in a, secretly located, armoured vehicle.

This story has many parallels with the thriller, "The Eagle has Landed" by author Jack Higgins. Many will recall that in the film version, the German paratroop commander, played by Michael Caine, was to abduct Winston Churchill from a remote country house. Fact and fiction do merge! In fact, much later, in September 2002, two unauthorised gliders did land on the Balmoral lawn, when the Queen and the Duke of Edinburgh were in residence. This, happily, was an emergency landing with no security risk.

Finally, on the 18 November 1944, General Franklyn (Commander in Chief CHQ Home Forces) wrote to the Colonel Douglas, Commander Auxiliary Units, informing him that the War Office had decided that, in view of the improved war situation, the Operational Branch of the Auxiliary Units should be stood down. Accordingly, as instructed, Colonel Douglas sent out the following letter of Stand-Down

"From:- Colonel F W R Douglas.
To:- The Members of Auxiliary Units – Operational Branch

The War Office has ordered that the Operational side of Auxiliary Units shall stand down! This is due to the greatly improved War situation and the strategic requirements of the movement.

I realise what joining Auxiliary Units has meant to you; so do the officers under my command. You were invited to do a job which would require more skill and coolness, more hard work and greater danger, than was demanded of any other voluntary organisation. In the event of "Action Stations" being ordered you knew well the kind of life you were in for. But that was in order; you were picked men; and others, including myself, knew that you would continue to fight whatever the conditions, with, or if necessary without, orders.

It now falls to me to tell you that your work has been appreciated and well carried out, and that your contract, for the moment, is at an end. I am grateful to you for the way you have trained in the last four years. So is the Regular Army. It was due to you that more divisions left this country to fight the battle of France; and it was due to your reputation for skill and determination that extra risk was taken – successfully as it turned out – in the defence arrangements of this country during that vital period. I congratulate you on this reputation and thank you for this voluntary effort.

In view of the fact that your lives depended on secrecy no public recognition will be possible. But those in the most responsible positions at General Headquarters, Home Forces, know what was done; and what would have been done had you been called upon. They know it well, as is emphasised in the attached letter from the Commander-in Chief. It will not be forgotten.

30 Nov 44	Colonel,
C/O G.P.O. HIGHWORTH,	Commander,
Nr. Swindon (Wilts).	Auxiliary Units.

The next important job was to collect all the weapons, ammunition, explosives and other stores from the 640 patrols. This proved to be a haphazard operation, both due to the secrecy of the organisation and the fact that the regular personnel had but all disappeared. There are many stories of former patrol members clearing woodland with forgotten explosives, together with the odd cache, secretly hidden, turning up most unexpectedly, many years later. Even today some former patrol members still possess their fighting knives, ammunition and other bits of equipment.

What to do with the underground bases? A question that must have exercised many a military brain. Whilst the element of secrecy regarding the very existence of Auxiliary Units had by now become somewhat diluted, there was still strong resistance to the location of OBs being revealed.

In most cases the personnel, who had built them, had moved onto other theatres of war and may have lost their lives. Anyhow, at the end of this long war, all most servicemen had on their minds was to get demobbed and go home. The only knowledge of the OBs was left with the individual patrol.

In an undated, top secret, report, believed to be 1944, the Commander, Auxiliary Units, had speculated on the future of OBs:-

"Security. Another factor to be considered is that of security. Are Obs to be allowed to remain intact, empty and thrown open to the public? Some little while ago I know that it was considered desirable that the whole organisation, its functions, role and method should remain SECRET and pigeon-holed in the War Office just in case….

If the Obs with their ingenious doors and camouflaged entrances are to be become local sights security has gone for good. On the other hand if the entrances are filled in or 'blown' security will not suffer and there would be the additional advantage that however much an ex-auxiliary wanted to 'shoot a line' he would not be believed unless he could show something and a heap of earth is most unconvincing.

It is probable that most patrols could deal with their own with supervision. Special Duties OBs however would have to be dealt with by regular personnel."

No precise instruction to Auxiliary Units on this issue has yet to be found. But, as far as the East Riding is concerned, most appeared to have been destroyed by Royal Engineer demolition parties. Isolated cases have missed the treatment, but all Special Duties OBs appear to be intact, with just the entrance being sealed.

7.2   No 33 North Bar Within, Beverley (right) the former premises of BM & E Thorpe, High Class Confectionery & Tobacconists. The upper floors and rear were used as the secret HQ of No 2 Region, Auxiliary Units in 1944. (Author's coll.)

115

8. THE FINAL CHAPTER

So as the Auxiliary Units closed down, the civilian patrol members continued with their day jobs, night-time being their normal operational duty. They were still constrained by the Official Secrets Act and they spoke little about the organisation. The regular personnel went back to their units to await demobilisation at the end of the war in 1945.

Unlike the other branches of the Home Services, Auxiliary Unit members were denied the Defence Medal. Their final stand-down letter from Col. Douglas clearly stated that *"In view of the fact that your lives depended on secrecy no public recognition will be possible"*. Their only reward was the issue of a small souvenir, enamelled lapel badge, with a crown and the numbers representing the three battalions.

After the war some units had a re-union. The East Riding had their county re-union in February 1946 at the Beverley Arms, which, by chance, was almost next door to the former No2 Region Auxiliary Unit's HQ at No 33 North Bar Within. A surviving copy of the menu shows that the toastmaster was Captain S Holmes (Commander No8 Group). Other persons proposing toasts were Lt F Byass (Commander No4 Group), Sgt W Massey (Patrol Leader, South Cave) and Captain Colley (Area Commander (North). How many attended is not known, this being the first and only re-union of the East Riding.

The existence of the organisation was a comparatively well kept secret, until the publication in 1968 of a book by American author David Lampe. His book entitled "The Last Ditch" was the first major work to describe the role and details of the Auxiliary Units. This was written without the secret background papers now readily available to researchers in the Public Record Office. It was, and still remains, the definitive book on the subject.

The publication of this book prompted a series of five articles in the Yorkshire Evening Post under the heading of INVASION 1940- YORKSHIRE'S SECRET SOLDIERS, written by Derek Naylor. These contained interviews with some senior commanders of the East Riding Auxiliary Units. Every one of those named has long since passed away, and therefore these testimonies have proved to be an invaluable source of information today.

It was another 27 years until the subject once again gained prominence in the media, with the launch of the Defence of Britain Project in 1995. This was a 5-year national project to locate, and record, all surviving 20th century defences within the United Kingdom. This revealed for the first time the surviving underground bases, which had long since been forgotten, and whose true identity had remained a well kept secret.

As well as a series of radio and television broadcasts, dealing with Auxiliary Units, two valuable booklets relating to the Sussex and Suffolk organisation found their way into print.

In 1994 the first national re-union was held, appropriately, at Coleshill when about sixty auxiliaries attended a commemorative lunch in the Church Hall. The sole representatives from the North were three stalwarts from the Bainton Patrol, namely Frank Byass, David Byass and John Elgey.

Other re-unions followed, in particular, those held by the Essex group at Colchester, arranged by the late Arthur Gabbitas, which attracted members nationally. The East Riding was usually represented by Charlie Mason (South Cave Patrol) and the author.

8.1 East Riding Auxiliary Unit Re-union on 27th February 1946. Copy of menu card courtesy of Frank Byass.

> <u>202 (G.H.Q.RESERVE)BATTALION HOME GUARD.</u>
>
> <u>OLD COMRADES REUNION DINNER.</u>
>
> <u>Beverley Arms Hotel.</u>
>
> <u>27th February, 1946.</u>
>
> This dinner is being held as an occasion of reunion. Together we have played our part towards the Victory which has been won, but the good comradeship which has existed will help us to retain our memories of fellowship.

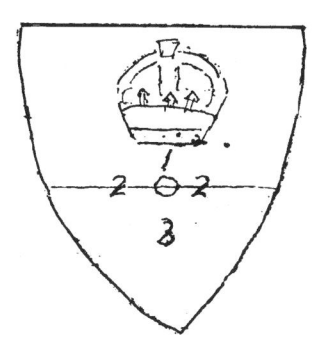

117

8.2   Auxiliary Units Reunion at the Museum of the British Resistance Organisation, Parham, Norfolk on 2 July 2000. (Author 2000)

8.3   Rev Peter Hollis and Charlie Mason at their own reunion at Sudbury, Suffolk, 1996. (Author)

8.4   TV Presenter Rory McGrath and the Author, at the South Dalton Control (Zero) Station entrance during the filming for BBC Knowledge Channel's History Fix series in 1999. (Author's coll.)

1997 saw the opening of the British Resistance Organisation Museum at the former Parham Military Airfield, which housed the 390th Bomber Group Memorial Air Museum. It organised the Millennium re-union held there on the 2nd July 2000. Described as the final re-union, it was attended by almost 160 persons, including 60 former Auxiliary Unit members. The Museum has also fronted the ongoing battle with Ministry of Defence to obtain the Defence Medal for all members.

The National Trust, at Coleshill, is also publicising its wartime role with exhibitions, and the re-opening of an underground observation base for public inspection. They have a special Book of Remembrance, commemorating some Auxiliary Units by the planting trees within the parkland. The East Riding Auxiliary Units are remembered by a walnut tree (No 22) which had been dedicated to them.

That would appear to be the end of the covert resistance movement. However, in the late 1950s 'Men in Grey Suits' were appearing on the south coast seeking out local trustworthy and 'weapon friendly' citizens who would be prepared to keep guns in their homes for a future national need. Nothing further was heard on this score, but the words of Major Oxenden in his, recently discovered, secret 1945 report on the Auxiliary Units, may now have some meaning, he wrote:

"The Unit has just evaporated, nothing now remains but a 20,000 word account of our history and final teaching, which I had the honour of writing, filed away in the secret archives of the W.O. until the next time that hostile troops are sitting on the other side of the channel...."

The Next Time!!

8.5 Page from the Coleshill Park Estate Tree Planting Book commemorating the service of the East Riding Auxiliary Units. (Author's coll.)

Coleshill Estate

A tree has been planted at Coleshill
On behalf of
Charles A. Mason
To commemorate the
East Riding of Yorkshire Auxiliary Units
(GHQ Home Forces 202 Battalion)
1940 - 1944

Appendix A

O.B. Discipline

1. General

Conversion of night into day fundamentally reverses mode of life. Patrol Leader's responsibility to ensure that efficiency is not lost through lack of foresight nor through unrealistic rehearsals. Lecture is based on assumption that O.B. is perfectly ventilated, camouflaged, and construction completed.

2. Food

Rations are already cooked, and can be served cold or warmed up to eating temperature. Ration Packs are for emergency use only, and must not be squandered, Patrol Leader must give out exact and equal rations, and not allow them to help themselves as they feel like it.

No frying is to be permitted on any account.

Any cooking of locally obtained meat and vegetables should be done whilst the Patrol is away at night, and so allow the O.B. to become well ventilated.

Patrols must eat to live, and not the reverse, and should therefore take pride in their economy of food rather then in extravagant meals.

Remember that there may be emergency demands, such as stray parties of one's own troops, and no one can say when food will again be obtained.

Water. Keep this sterilized and turned over.

3. Rum.

Seal up the jar after each time it is broached. Be scrupulously fair in its distribution, and not over lavish. Best issued on return from Patrol.

4. Smoking

This MUST be controlled, and 10-15 minutes in each hour must be sufficient. Remember it is not only a question of fresh air, but the give away of smoke fumes from the ventilator.

5. Sleep

It is essential to enforce "Lights Out" for about eight hours from dawn onwards. Existence otherwise becomes timeless, and nobody gets any proper rest, since there is always somebody talking or moving about.

6. Light

Although a brilliant petrol lamp gives a cheerful effect, it is a very doubtful benefit, as the glare, heat and noise are unconsciously tiring.

The hurricane lantern throws shadows where they are least wanted, and are apt to smell.

The ordinary candle is worth more consideration, especially with white painted walls.

The outlet must be continually checked for "Black Out"

7. Care of Arms and Stores, etc

Dirt and Damp chief enemies. Constant care and cleaning necessary. Plenty of opportunity to do so, and should be a routine matter.

Cleanliness of O.B. essential – not only for care of arms, etc, but psychologically.

Respirators should be worn periodically and exposed to the air.

8. Mental Dullness

This is inevitable, and must be relieved by mental gymnastics (pelmanism, etc) and by a few minutes rest in the open air on emerging from O.B. Extinguish all lights for 10 minutes before emerging so that men are not bewildered by contrast. Give each man a specific task in O.B. maintenance so that he has something definite to do. Cleanliness is a good antidote.

Beware of pessimism and despondency, which are the natural outcome of failure and casualties. Ill feeling, which may arise from some mistake of Patrol, should be checked.

9. Physical Fitness

Our work requires highest state of fitness. Patrol Leader must check up, and not allow unfit men to proceed on duty. Remember that any normal functions will be upset by inverted mode of life. Have as supply of Health Salts or pills.

First Aid sets must be kept clean and a personal check of morphia tablets made by the Patrol Leader.

See the clothes are kept properly dried.

10. General Amenities

Playing cards, sealed tins of cigarettes, Dart Board, Radio Set.

Bedroom slippers or canvas shoes, lavatory paper, matches, pencils, needles and thread, bootlaces, soap, corks, vacuum flask.

24 hours of an Auxiliary's Life (Winter)

1430 Reveille
1515 Meal – Hot tea – cold food.
1600 – 1700   Clean O.B., wash up, make up beds. Inspect weapons, stores, equipment.
1700 – 1800   Stand easy – smoking allowed for 15 minutes
1800 – 1900   Meal – hot tea – cold food.
1900 – 2030   Prepare for night patrol.
2030 – 2045   Emerge and rest in open air.
2045 – 0545   Patrol – During absence, hot meal is cooked by next day's Observer.
0600   Hot meal – after which observer moves to his task.
0700   Lights Out."

Appendix B

Sgt. Bill Massey's instruction to his South Cave Patrol on their changing role in 1944.

I) In the event of a Raid by Enemy Airborne Troops we are to be attached to the South Cave
H G Coy as a Reconnaissance Patrol.

II) Preliminary warnings of an impending raid will be given by the word '**bouncer**'. All should see that their gear is ready for mustering at a moment's notice on receipt of this.

On receipt of the word '**bugbear**', all will make their way to the mustering point as quickly as possible.

III) **Call Out -** This has been worked out in conjunction with the South Cave Home Guard. Details below

Ernie Colbeck}	will be informed	by Lt Vyse & Jack Cross}
Gordon Watson	"	by Lt Danby
Ben Taylor	"	by The Sergeant Major S. Cave HQ
Charlie Mason	"	by Ted Childs & myself on the way to the mustering point

IV) **Mustering Point -** *Wooden Hut at back of Bear Inn. There we will received instructions from Lt. Vyse.*

V) **Equipment -** *all will wear Battledress, & F S Caps, & will bring either the rifle or Sten Gun that has been issued to them. Ammo will be provided by S. Cave H G. Sten Gunners will bring 2 magazines & filler. We are also supposed to bring Respirators. S. Cave H G are obtaining Tin Hats & Gas Capes for us. I will bring a supply of camouflage cream.*

VI) **Food -** *all will make up a pack of food sufficient to last them for 24 hours. After this period, Army Rations will be available (Note: - this arrangement applies to the South Cave HG also)*

VII) **General**

I) If you haven't already done so, it would be a good plan to get all your gear together see that it is in good order & also see that these things that, are supposed to work DO work. Get your weapon – (I mean your Rifle or Sten Gun) – into 1st Class order, it may be your best-friend for a time.

II) Wear your gear & equipment when you have a spare moment and see that you can carry it all comfortably & effectively.

III) I have details of the S Cave Battle Plan – O.P's, moving Patrols etc, and at the earliest opportunity we will all make ourselves familiar with this.

IV) Lt Vyse has suggested that the Patrol should be 'on view' to his South Cave HG at an early date to avoid unfortunate incidents later on. This 'Private Exhibition' will be laid on at the earliest convenience.

· BEN TAYLOR.

Programme for February 1944

Feb.	Day	Subject	Details
4.	F.	Test of Equipment in O.B.	Meet. West End of Weedley Tunnel. 8 p.m.
5.	Sun.	Daylight Movement up Low Hunsley.	East End " " " 10 a.m.
7.	M.	Further Test of O.B. Equipment (if Req'd) or. Night Scheme to be arranged by Gordon Watson.	As for Feb 4th or Fox & Coney 8 p.m.
	F.	Lecture "Fire Orders" at Welton.	Meet. with Bykes, Fox & Coney. 7.30 p.m.
13	Sun.	Sniping Practice with Moving Target Gear & 'Fire Orders'.	Beverley Clump. 10. a.m.
14.	M.	Council of War for Friday Night Operation at Newport.	Gordon Watson's House. 8.p.m. (If Mrs Watson is in agreement).
	F.	Night Scheme. v. Newport HG.	Details Later.
	Sun.	Communications Route between South & North Cave.	Meet. West End of Weedley Tunnel 10. a.m.
	M.	Night Firing with Sten Guns at Moving Targets.	Meet. Gordon Watson's House 8 p.m.
	F.	First Aid Lecture. Welton.	Meet. Fox & Coney. 7.30.p.m.
	Sun.	Demolition Exercises.	Details Later.
	M.	Night Scheme in Drewton Area.	Meet. West End of Weedley Tunnel 8. p.m.

E.J.Massey
1.2.44.

9.1 South Cave Patrol's Training Programme for February 1944. Note the meeting at Gordon Watson's house depended on 'Mrs Watson's agreement'! (Author's coll.)

```
                    AUXILIARY UNITS.
                    G.H.Q. Home Forces.

        1940                                    1944


                            1994
                    COMMEMORATIVE LUNCHEON
                        The Church Hall
                          COLESHILL
                       25th.October 1994

         Highworth Fertilisers - Do their stuff unseen -
                    Until you see RESULTS!


                            MENU
                   Cream of Vegetable Soup or
                       Egg Mayonnaise or
                      Chicken Liver Pate
                          *******
      Roast Wiltshire Turkey, Cranberry Sauce and Stuffing or
            Roast Rib of Beef with Yorkshire Pudding
                   Chef's selection of Vegetables
                          *******
                      Choice of Sweet or
                      Cheese and Biscuits
                          *******
                       Coffee with Cream
                          *******

30 Nov.1944                                    c/o GPO Highworth.
..... I realise what joining Auxiliary Units has meant to you .....
You were invited to do a job which would require more skill and
coolness, more hard work and greater danger than was demanded of any
other voluntary organisation. In the event of "Action Stations"
being ordered you knew well the kind of life you were in for.
But that was in order; you were picked men, and others, including
myself knew that you would continue to fight whatever the conditions,
with, or, if necessary without orders.  ..... In view of the fact that
your lives depended on secrecy, no public recognition will be possible.
But those in the most responsible positions at G.H.Q. Home Forces
know what was done, and what would have been done, if you had been
called upon.
               They know it well. It will not be forgotten.
                              (signed) Frank W.R.Douglas.
                              Colonel.Commander Auxiliary Units.
                          *******
                    John Tohhem Elgey
                    ------------------
                    served in the Auxiliary Units
                              from
                    1940              to    1944
```

9.2 Commemorative menu of the Auxiliary Units Re-unions at Coleshill on 25th October 1994. This has John Elgey's name who attended with Frank and David Byass, all former Bainton Patrol members. (John Elgey coll.)

References

'**The Last Ditch**' by David Lampe, published in 1968, was without doubt the starting point for all research.

The primary references were Public Record Office documents WO199/294, WO 199/738, WO 199/937, WO 1426PTZ, WO 199/1517 and WO 199/3389.

The East Riding County Archives contain only the Home Guard Company Registers.

The Auxiliary Units special training manuals, Calendar 1937, Calendar 1938, and the Countryman's Diary 1939 are also a major source of information on sabotage and the use of explosives.

The University of Hull's Metcalfe Collection contains a series of German maps, photographs and other details dated 1940-1942, covering an area from the River Humber to the River Tay, entitled '**Military Geographical Targets**'

The following newspapers/periodicals have also provided much reference material:-

Hull Daily Mail	– April 16 1966
Yorkshire Evening Post	– May 1968
Malton Gazette & Herald	– Jan 10 1991
Military Illustrated	– August 1992
Country Life	– December 1992
Sunday Express	– November 6 1994
Sunday Express	– March 12 1995
The Times	– September 7 1996
Daily Mail	– September 7 1996
The Northern Echo	– September 14-16 1996
Defence Lines	– November 1996
Lincolnshire Auxiliary Units Newsletter No2	– April 1998

Select Bibliography

Against All Odds - The British Army 1939-40 - National Army Museum 1990

Alexander, Colin - Ironside's Line - Historic Military Press 1999

Angel, Stewart -The Secret Sussex Resistance - Middleton Press 1996

Beyts, GHB - The King's Salt - Privately Published - revisited 1996

British War Production, 1939-1945 - The Times 1945

Brophy, John – Britain's Home Guard – Harrop & Co 1945

Cocks, A E - Churchill's Secret Army etc - The Book Guild 1992

Collier, Basil - The Defence of the United Kingdom - HMSO 1957

Croft, Andrew - A Talent for Adventure - Spa 1991

Cruikshank, Dan - Invasion, Defending Britain from Attack - Boxtree 2001

Dewing, Geoff - Suffolk's Secret Army 1940-44 - Privately published 1996

Dobinson, Colin - Twentieth Century Fortifications in England - Volume X Airfield defences in WWII - Council for British Archaeology 2000

Dunning, John - Bishop Burton and Its People - Highgate Publications 1992

Fleming, Peter - Invasion 1940, - Rupert Hart Davis 1957
(also published under title, Operation Sea Lion, Pan Books 1975)

Gilbert, Adrian - Britain Invaded - Century 1990

Glover, Michael - Invasion Scare 1940 - Leo Cooper 1990

Graves, Charles - The Home Guard of Britain - Hutchinson & Co 1943

Lampe, David - The Last Ditch - Cassel 1968

Leigh-Lye, Terry - A Century of Boxing - Mayflower 1971

Lowry, Bernard & Wilkes, Mick - The Mercian Marquis - Logaston Press 2002

Oxendon, Major R V - Auxiliary Units History & Achievement 1940-44 - BRO Museum 1998

Schellenberg, Captain Walter, - Invasion 1940 - St Ermins Press 2000

Shaw, Eddie - A Saboteur in War Time - Pavitt Publications ND

Stevens, Gordon - And All the Kings Men - Pan Books 1990

Warwicker, John, Editor - With Britain in Mortal Danger - Cerberus 2002

Wheatley, Ronald - Operation Sea Lion - Oxford Paperbacks 1958

Whittacker, Len - Some Talk of Private Armies - Albanium Publishing 1990

Wilkinson, Astley J B - Gubbins and SOE - Leo Cooper 1993